χαλωσορίζες!

Just Enough **Greek**

D. L. Ellis, H. Rapi

Pronunciation **Dr. J. Baldwin**

PASSPORT BOOKS

Trade Imprint of National Textbook Company
Lincolnwood, Illinois U.S.A.

The publishers would like to thank the
National Tourist Organisation of Greece for their help
during the preparation of this book

1986 Printing

This edition first published in 1983 by Passport Books, Trade
Imprint of National Textbook Company, 4255 West Touhy
Avenue, Lincolnwood, Illinois 60646-1975 U.S.A.

567890RD 98765

Contents

Using the phrase book

- This phrase book is designed to help you get by in Greece, to get what you want or need. It concentrates on the simplest but most effective way you can express these needs in an unfamiliar language.
- The CONTENTS on p. 5 gives you a good idea of which section to consult for the phrase you need.
- The INDEX on p. 155 gives more detailed information about where to look for your phrase.
- When you have found the right page you will be given:
  either – the exact phrase
  or – help in making up a suitable sentence
  and – help to get the pronunciation right
- The English sentences in **bold type** will be useful for you in a variety of different situations, so they are worth learning by heart. (See also DO IT YOURSELF, p. 142.)
- Wherever possible you will find help in understanding what Greek people are saying to *you*, in reply to your questions.
- If you want to practise the basic nuts and bolts of the language further, look at the DO IT YOURSELF section starting on p. 142.
- Note especially these three sections:
  Everyday expressions, p. 14
  Shop talk, p. 58
  Public notices, p. 119
  You are sure to want to refer to them most frequently.
- Once abroad, remember to make good use of the local tourist offices (see p. 27).

North American addresses:

Greek National Tourist Office
Olympic Tower
645 Fifth Avenue
New York, NY 10022
(212) 421-5777

Greek National Tourist Office
611 W. Sixth Street
Suite 1998
Los Angeles, CA 90017
(213) 626-6696

Greek National Tourist Office
2 Place Ville Marie
Esso Plaza
Montreal, Quebec
Canada
H3B2C9
(514) 535-8711

A note on the pronunciation system and the Greek alphabet

In traveler's phrase books there is usually a pronunciation section which tries to teach English-speaking tourists how to correctly pronounce the language of the country they are visiting. This is based on the belief that in order to be understood, the speaker must have an accurate, authentic accent—that he must pronounce every last word letter-perfectly.

The authors of this book, on the other hand, wanted to devise a workable and usable pronunciation system. So they had to face the fact it is absolutely impossible for an average speaker of English who has no technical training in phonetics and phonetic transcription systems (which includes 98% of all the users of this book!) to reproduce the sounds of a foreign language with perfect accuracy, just from reading a phonetic transcription, cold—no prior background in the language. We also believe that you don't have to have perfect pronunciation in order to make yourself understood in a foreign country. After all, natives you run into will take into account that you are foreigners, and visitors, and more than likely they will feel gratified by your efforts to communicate and will probably go out of their way to try to understand you. They may even help you, and correct you, in a friendly manner. We have found, also, that visitors to a foreign country are not usually concerned with perfect pronunciation—they just want to get their message across, to communicate!

With this in mind, we have designed a pronunciation system which is of the utmost simplicity to use. This system does not attempt to give an accurate—but also problematical and tedious—representation of the sound system of the language, but instead uses common sound and letter combinations in English which are the closest to the sounds in the foreign language. In this way, the sentences transcribed for pronunciation should be read as naturally as possible, as if they were ordinary English. In no way does the user have to attempt to make the words sound "foreign." So, while to yourselves you will sound as if you are speaking ordinary English—or at least making ordinary English sounds—you will at the same time be making yourselves understood in another language. And, as the saying goes, practice makes perfect, so it is probably a good idea to repeat aloud to yourselves several times the phrases you think you are going to use, before you actually use them. This will give you greater confidence, and will also help in making yourself understood.

In Greek it is important to stress or emphasize the syllables in *italics*, just as you would if we were to take as an English example: Little Jack Horner sat in the corner. Here we have ten syllables, but only four stresses. This is particularly important in Greek, as meaning can be dependent on stress and many words will be completely unintelligible to a Greek unless the stress is put in the correct place.

Of course you may enjoy trying to pronounce a foreign language as well as possible, and the present system is a good way to start. However, since it uses only the sounds of English, you will very soon need to depart from it as you imitate the sounds you hear the native speaker produce and relate them to the spelling of the other language.

In the case of Greek there is a new alphabet to be learned which at first sight is likely to appear rather strange. However, if you are able to spend a little time studying it, you will find that it is in fact much simpler than our own alphabet! There are only twenty-four letters and the rules relating to their pronunciation are quite simple and regular. If you follow the guidelines below, you should be able to produce an intelligible rendering of any Greek word you see.

Printed	Handwritten	Name	Pronunciation
A α	*A a*	alfa	*a* as in f*a*ther, e.g. μαῦρος (m*a*vros) black
B β	*β b*	v*ee*ta	*v* as in *v*an, e.g. βαλίτσα (*v*aleetsa) suitcase
Γ γ	*Γ f*	g*a*ma	throaty *g*; *g* in *g*uild is quite acceptable, e.g. γάλα (g*a*la) milk. Before ε, η, ι, υ it becomes *y* e.g. γιά (*y*a) for
Δ δ	*Δ f*	d*e*lta	*th* as in *th*is and bro*th*er, e.g. δύο (*th*ee-o) two
E ε	*E ε*	eps*ee*lon	*e* as in g*e*t, e.g. ἐδῶ (*e*tho) here
Z ζ	*Z J*	z*ee*ta	*z* as in *z*oo, e.g. ζεστός (*z*estoss) hot
H η	*H η*	*ee*ta	*ee* as in m*ee*t, e.g. ἡλεκτρικό (*ee*lektreeko) electricity supply
Θ θ	*Θ ϑ*	th*ee*ta	*th* as in *th*in, e.g. θέλω (*th*el-o) I want
I ι	*I ι*	e*ee*ota	*ee* as in m*ee*t, e.g. σπίτι (sp*ee*tee) house

Printed	Handwritten		Name	Pronunciation
Κ κ	κ	κ	kapa	*k* as in *k*itten, e.g. καί (keh) and
Λ λ	Λ	λ	lambda	*l* as in *l*ive, e.g. λυπᾶμαι (leepam-eh) I am sorry
Μ μ	Μ	μ	mee	*m* as in *m*y, e.g. μέ (meh) with
Ν ν	Ν	ν	nee	*n* as in *n*ever, e.g. ναί (neh) yes
Ξ ξ	Ξ	ξ	ksee	*ks* as in tri*ck*s, e.g. ἕξι (eksee) six
Ο ο	Ο	ο	omeekron	*o* as in h*o*t, e.g. ὄνομα (onomah) name
Π π	Π	ω	pee	*p* as in *p*ie, e.g. πέντε (pendeh) five
Ρ ρ	Ρ	ρ	ro	a semi-rolled *r* as in *r*ed, e.g. ρετσίνα (retseenah) resinated wine
Σ σ ς	Σ	ς	seegma	*s* as in *s*end, e.g. στῆθος (steethos) breast. Before β, γ, δ it becomes *z* but this is not very common. The form ς is used only at the end of a word
Τ τ	Τ	τ	taf	*t* as in *t*op, e.g. Τρίτη (treetee) Tuesday
Υ υ	Υ	υ	eepseelon	*ee* as in m*ee*t, e.g. μπύρα (beera) beer
Φ φ	Φ	φ	fee	*f* as in *f*our, e.g. φιλμ (film) film
Χ χ	Χ	χ	hee	*ch* as in lo*ch* or if you can't make this sound, a fairly forceful *h* as in *h*elp, e.g. χρόνὸς (hronoss) year
Ψ ψ	ψ	ψ	psee	*ps* as in to*ps*, e.g. ψάρι (psaree) fish
Ω ω	Ω	ω	omega	*o* as in h*o*t, e.g. ὥρα (orah) hour, time

You have probably noticed that some of the letters are pronounced alike. They are Ηη Ιι Υυ pronounced *ee* as in m*ee*t, agr*ee* and Οο Ωω pronounced *o* as in h*o*t.

COMBINATIONS OF LETTERS

αι   *e* as in g*e*t, e.g. καί (keh) and

αυ   *av* as in h*av*e, e.g. αὔριο (*av*reeo) tomorrow, but before
     voiceless consonants θ, κ, ξ, π, σ, τ, φ, χ, ψ pronounced *af*,
     e.g. αὐτό (*af*to) this

ει   *ee* as in m*ee*t, e.g. τρεῖς (tr*ee*ss) three

ευ   *ev* as in *ev*ent, e.g. Εὐρώπη (*ev*ropee) Europe, but before
     voiceless consonants θ, κ, ξ, π, σ, τ, φ, χ, ψ pronounced *ef*,
     e.g. εὐχαριστῶ (*ef*-har-eesto) thank you

οι   *ee* as in m*ee*t, e.g. κοινός (k*ee*noss) public

ου   *oo* as in f*oo*l, e.g. μπουκάλι (book*a*lee) bottle

γγ   *ng* as in a*ng*le, e.g. Ἀγγλία (a*ng*leea) England

γκ   *g* as in g*e*t, e.g. γκαρσόν (garso*n*) waiter, but in the middle
     of a word *ng*, e.g. ἄγκυρα (a*ng*eera) anchor

γχ   *nh* as in e*nh*ance, e.g. μέ συγχωρεῖτε (meh see*nh*oreeteh)
     excuse me

μπ   *b* as in *b*ar, e.g. μπάρ (*b*ar) bar, but in the middle of a word
     sometimes *mb* as in la*mb*a (lamba) light bulb

ντ   *d* as in *d*ot, e.g. ντομάτα (*d*omata) tomato, but in the middle
     of a word *nd*, e.g. πέντε (pe*nd*eh) five

Note that the ' ', used where a word begins with a vowel have *no*
function in pronunciation and must therefore be ignored. The three
marks ` ´ ῀ all show one and the same thing, i.e. which syllable
carries stress; they have no other function.

καλή ἐπιτυχία!
kalee epeeteeheea

Mainland Greece

Mainland Greece and the islands

Everyday expressions

[See also 'Shop talk', p. 58]

Hello	Γειά σας
	yassas
Good morning ⎤	Καλημέρα
Good day ⎦	kal-eemehra
Good afternoon (after siesta) ⎤	Καλησπέρα
Good evening ⎦	kaleespera
Good night	Καληνύκτα
	kal-eeneekta
Goodbye	Γειά σας
	yassas
See you later	Θά σᾶς δῶ ἀργότερα
	tha sas tho argot-ehra
Yes	Ναί
	neh
Please	Παρακαλῶ
	parakalo
Yes, please	Ναί, παρακαλῶ
	neh, parakalo
Great!	ὡραῖα!
	oreh-a
Thank you	Εὐχαριστῶ
	ef-har-eesto
Thank you very much	Εὐχαριστῶ πάρα πολύ
	ef-har-eesto para pol-ee
That's right	Σωστό
	sosto
No	Ὄχι
	o-hee
No, thank you	Ὄχι, εὐχαριστῶ
	o-hee ef-har-eesto
I disagree	Διαφωνῶ
	thee-af-on-o
Excuse me ⎤	Συγγνώμη
Sorry ⎦	seeg-nom-ee
Don't mention it ⎤	Δέν πειράζει
That's OK ⎦	then peeraz-ee

That's good ⎤ I like it ⎦	Αὐτό εἶναι καλό afto eeneh kalo
That's no good ⎤ I don't like it ⎦	Δέν μ' ἀρέσει then mar-es-ee
I know	Ξέρω ksehro
I don't know	Δέν ξέρω then ksehro
It doesn't matter	Δέν πειράζει then peeraz-ee
Where's the toilet, please?	Ποῦ εἶναι ἡ τουαλέτα, παρακαλῶ; poo een-eh ee too-al-eh-ta parakalo
How much is that? [point]	Πόσο κάνει ἐκεῖνο; posso kan-ee ekeeno
Is the service included?	Εἶναι μέ τό σερβίς; eeneh meh toh sehr-veess
Do you speak English?	Μιλᾶτε Ἀγγλικά; meelat-eh angleeka
I'm sorry . . .	Λυπᾶμαι ἀλλά . . . leepam-eh alla . . .
I don't speak Greek	δέν μιλῶ ἑλληνικά then meelo elleen-eeka
I only speak a little Greek	μιλῶ μόνο λίγα ἑλληνικά meelo mono leeg-a elleen-eeka
I don't understand	δέν καταλαβαίνω then kat-alav-en-o
Please can you . . .	Σᾶς παρακαλῶ, μπορεῖτε νά . . . sas parakalo, boreeteh na . . .
repeat that?	τό ἐπαναλάβετε αὐτό; toh ep-an-alav-et-eh afto
speak more slowly?	μιλᾶτε πιό ἀργά; meelat-eh pee-o arga
write it down?	τό γράψετε; toh grapset-eh
What is this called in Greek? [point]	Πῶς τό λέτε στά Ἑλληνικά; poss toh let-eh sta elleen-eeka

Crossing the border

ESSENTIAL INFORMATION

- Don't waste time before you leave rehearsing what you're going to say to the border officials – the chances are that you won't have to say anything at all, especially if you travel by air.
- It's more useful to check that you have your documents handy for the journey: passport, tickets, money, travellers' cheques, insurance documents, driving licence and car registration documents.
- Look for these signs:
  ΤΕΛΩΝΕΙΟΝ (customs)
  ΣΥΝΟΡΑ (border)
  [For further signs and notices, see p. 119]
- You may be asked routine questions by the customs officials [see below]. If you have to give personal details see 'Meeting people', p. 18. The other important answer to know is 'Nothing': Τίποτα (teepota).

ROUTINE QUESTIONS

Passport?	Διαβατήριο; thee-av-ateerio
Insurance?	Ἀσφάλεια; as-fal-ya
Registration document? (logbook)	Ἄδεια κυκλοφορίας; athia keek-loforee-ass
Ticket, please	Τό εἰσιτήριο σας, παρακαλῶ toh eess-eeteerio sas parakalo
Have you anything to declare?	Ἔχετε νά δηλώσετε τίποτα; eh-het-eh na thee-loss-et-eh teepota
Where are you going?	Ποῦ πηγαίνετε; poo peeg-en-et-eh
How long are you staying?	Πόσο θά μείνετε; posso tha meenet-eh
Where have you come from?	Ἀπό ποῦ ἤρθατε; apo poo eerthat-eh

You may also have to fill in forms which ask for:

surname	επώνυμο
first name	όνομα
date of birth	ἡμερομηνία γεννήσεως
address	διεύθυνση
nationality	ἐθνικότης
profession	ἐπάγγελμα
passport number	ἀριθμός διαβατηρίου
issued at	ἐκδοθέν εἰς
place of birth	τόπος γεννήσεως
signature	ὑπογραφή

Meeting people

[See also 'Everyday expressions', p. 14]

Breaking the ice

Hello	Γειά σας
	yassas
Good morning	Καλημέρα
	kal-eemehra
How are you?	Πῶς εἴστε;
	poss eess-teh
Pleased to meet you	Χαίρω πολύ
	hehr-o pol-*ee*
I am here . . .	Εἶμαι ἐδῶ . . .
	*ee*meh eth-*o* . . .
on holiday	γιά διακοπές
	ya thee-ak-opess
on business	γιά δουλειά
	ya thool-y*a*
Can I offer you . . .	Μπορῶ νά σᾶς προσφέρω . . .
	boro na sas pross-fehro . . .
a drink?	ἕνα ποτό;
	enna pot-*o*
a cigarette?	ἕνα τσιγάρο;
	enna tseegar-*o*
a cigar?	ἕνα ποῦρο;
	enna p*oo*-ro
Are you staying long?	Θά μείνετε πολύ;
	tha meenet-eh pol-*ee*

Name

What's your name?	Πῶς λέγεσται;
	poss leg-es-teh
My name is . . .	Μέ λένε . . .
	meh len-eh . . .

Family

Are you married?	Εἴστε παντρεμένος/παντρεμένη;*
	*ees-teh pandrem-en-oss/ pandrem-en-ee**
I am ...	Εἴμαι ...
	eemeh ...
married	παντρεμένος/παντρεμένη*
	*pandrem-en-oss/pandrem-en-ee**
single	ἀνύπαντρος/ἀνύπαντρη*
	*an-eepandr-oss/an-eepandr-ee**
This is ...	Ἀπό ἐδῶ ...
	apo eth-o ...
my wife	ἡ συζυγός μου
	ee seezeegozmoo
my husband	ὁ συζυγός μου
	o seezeegozmoo
my son	ὁ γυιός μου
	o yozmoo
my daughter	ἡ κόρη μου
	ee koreemoo
my (boy)friend	ὁ φίλος μου
	o feelozmoo
my (male) colleague	ὁ συνάδελφος μου
	o seen-athelf-ozmoo
my (female) colleague	ἡ συνάδελφος μου
	ee seen-athelf-ozmoo
Do you have any children?	Ἔχετε παιδιά;
	eh-het-eh peth-ya
I have ...	Ἔχω ...
	eh-ho ...
one daughter	μία κόρη
	mee-a koree
one son	ἕνα γυιό
	enna yo
two daughters	δύο κόρες
	thee-o koress
three sons	τρεῖς γυιούς
	treess yooss
No, I haven't any children	Ὄχι, δέν ἔχω παιδιά
	o-hee, then eh-ho peth-ya

*For men use the first alternative, for women the second.

Where you live

Are you Greek?	Εἴστε Ἕλληνας/Ἑλληνίδα;*
	ees-theh el*leenas*/elleen*eetha**
I am ...	Εἴμαι ...
	*ee*meh ...
American	'Αμερικανός/'Αμερικανίδα
	amerikan-*oss*/amerikan-*eetha**
English	Ἐγγλέζος/Ἐγγλέζα
	englez-*oss*/englez-*a**

[For other nationalities, see p. 136]

Where are you from?

I am ...	Εἴμαι ...
	*ee*meh ...
from London	ἀπό τό Λονδῖνο
	apo toh lon-th*eeno*
from England	ἀπό τήν 'Αγγλία
	apo teen anglee-*a*

[For other countries see p. 134]

from the north	ἀπό τό βορρᾶ
	apo toh vorr*a*
from the south	ἀπό τό νότο
	apo toh not-*o*
from the east	ἀπό τήν ἀνατολή
	apo teen anatol*ee*
from the west	ἀπό τή δύση
	apo tee th*eessee*
from the centre	ἀπό τό κέντρο
	apo toh k*endro*

*For men use the first alternative, for women the second.

For the businessman and woman

I'm from . . . (firm's name)	Εἶμαι ἀπό . . . *eemeh apo* . . .
I have an appointment with . . .	Ἔχω ραντεβοῦ μέ . . . *eh-ho randevoo meh* . . .
May I speak to . . .?	Μπορῶ νά μιλήσω στό . . .; *boro na meeleeso sto* . . .
This is my card	Ὁρίστε ἡ κάρτα μου *oreest-eh ee karta moo*
I'm sorry I'm late	Μέ συγχωρεῖτε πού ἄργησα *meh seenhor-eet-eh poo arg-eessa*
Can I fix another appointment?	Μπορῶ νά κλείσω ἄλλο ραντεβοῦ; *boro na kleeso allo randevoo*
I'm staying at the hotel (Delphi)	Μένω στό ξενοδοχεῖο (Δελφοί) *men-o sto ksen-otho-hee-o (Delphi)*
I'm staying in (Stadium) Street	Μένω στήν ὁδό (Σταδίου) *men-o steen otho (stathee-oo)*

Asking the way

ESSENTIAL INFORMATION

● Keep a look out for all these place names as you will find them on shops, maps and notices.

WHAT TO SAY

Excuse me, please	Μέ συγχωρεῖτε, παρακαλῶ
	meh seenhor-eet-eh parakalo
How do I get . . .	Πῶς μπορῶ νά πάω . . .
	poss boro na pa-o . . .
to Athens?	στήν 'Αθήνα;
	steen atheena
to Ermou Street?	στήν ὁδό Ἑρμοῦ;
	steen otho ehrmoo
to the Hotel Caravel?	στό ξενοδοχεῖο Καραβέλ;
	sto ksen-otho-hee-o karavel
to the airport?	στό ἀεροδρόμιο;
	sto ehr-othrom-yo
to the beach?	στή παραλία;
	stee paraleea
to the bus station?	στή στάση λεωφορείου;
	stee stassee leh-oforee-oo
to the historic site?	στό ἱστορικό μνημεῖο;
	sto eestoreeko mneemee-o
to the market?	στήν ἀγορά;
	steen agora
to the police station?	στήν ἀστυνομία;
	steen asteen-omee-a
to the port?	στό λιμάνι;
	sto leeman-ee
to the post office?	στό ταχυδρομεῖο;
	sto ta-hee-thromee-o
to the railway station?	στό σιδηροδρομικό σταθμό;
	sto see-theerothrom-eeko stathmo
to the sports stadium?	στό στάδιο;
	sto stathio

to the tourist information office?	στό γραφεῖο πληροφοριῶν γιά τουρίστες; sto grafee-o pleerof-oree-on ya tooreest-ess
to the town centre?	στό κέντρο τῆς πόλης; sto kendro teess pol-eess
to the town hall?	στό δημαρχεῖο; sto theem-ar-hee-o
Excuse me, please	Μέ συγχωρεῖτε, παρακαλῶ meh seenhor-eet-eh parakalo
Is there . . . near by?	Ὑπάρχει ἐδῶ κοντά . . . eepar-hee eth-o konda . . .
an art gallery	πινακοθήκη; peen-akoth-eekee
a baker's	ἀρτοποιεῖο; artop-ee-ee-o
a bank	τράπεζα; trap-ez-a
a bar	μπάρ; bar
a botanical garden	βοτανικός κῆπος; vot-an-eekoss keeposs
a bus stop	στάση λεωφορείου; stassee leh-oforee-oo
a butcher's	κρεοπωλεῖο; kreh-opolee-o
a café	καφενεῖο kafen-eeo
a cake and coffee shop	ζαχαροπλαστεῖο; za-har-oplastee-o
a campsite	κατασκήνωση; kata-skeenossee
a car park	πάρκιγκ; parking
a change bureau	γραφεῖο συναλλάγματος; grafee-o seenal-agmat-oss
a chemist's	φαρμακεῖο; farma-kee-o
a church	ἐκκλησία; ek-leessee-a
a cinema	σινεμά; seenema

Is there . . . near by?
Υπάρχει ἐδῶ κοντά . . .
eepar-hee eth-o konda . . .

a concert hall
αἴθουσα συναυλιῶν;
eh-thoossa seen-avli-on

a delicatessen
ἐδωδιμοπωλεῖο;
eth-oth-eemopolee-o

a dentist's
ὀδοντιατρεῖο;
othondi-atree-o

a department store
μεγάλο ἐμπορικό κατάστημα;
meh-gal-o emboreeko katasteema

a disco
ντισκοτέκ;
discoteque

a doctor's surgery
ἰατρεῖο;
ee-atree-o

a dry-cleaner's
στεγνοκαθαριστήριο;
stegno-kathar-eesteerio

a fishmonger's
ψαράδικο;
psarath-eeko

a garage (for repairs)
συνεργεῖο;
seenehr-geeo

a hairdresser's
κομμωτήριο;
kommot-eerio

a greengrocer's
μανάβικο;
manav-eeko

a grocer's
μπακάλικο;
bakal-eeko

a hardware shop
μαγαζί μέ σιδηρικά;
magaz-ee meh seeth-eeree-ka

a hospital
νοσοκομεῖο;
nosokomee-o

a hotel
ξενοδοχεῖο;
ksen-otho-hee-o

a laundry
καθαριστήριο;
kathar-eesteerio

a museum
μουσεῖο;
moossee-o

a newsagent's
περίπτερο;
peh-reeptero

a nightclub
νάϊτ κλάμπ;
night club

a petrol station
βενζινάδικο;
venzeen-atheeko

a postbox	γραμματοκιβώτιο; grammatok-eevot-yo
a toilet	τουαλέτα; too-al-eh-ta
a restaurant	ἑστιατόριο; estee-atorio
a snack bar	σνάκ μπάρ; snack bar
a sports ground	γήπεδο; yee-pehtho
a supermarket	σούπερ μαρκέτ; supermarket
a sweet shop (kiosk)	περίπτερο; peh-reeptero
a swimming pool	πισίνα; pee-seena
a taxi stand	πιάτσα γιά ταξί; pee-atsa ya taksee
a public telephone	τηλέφωνο; teelef-ono
a theatre	θέατρο; theh-atro
a tobacconist's kiosk	περίπτερο; peh-reeptero
a travel agent's	πρακτορείο ταξιδιῶν; praktoree-o takseethee-on
a youth hostel	ξενῶν νεότητος; ksen-on neh-ot-eetoss
a zoo	ζωολογικός κῆπος; zo-olog-eekoss keeposs

DIRECTIONS

- Asking where a place is, or if a place is near by, is one thing; making sense of the answer is another.
- Here are some of the most important directions and replies.

Left	Ἀριστερά areesteh-ra
Right	Δεξιά theksya
Straight on	Ἴσια eesia

There	Ἐκεῖ ek-*ee*
First left/right	Ὁ πρῶτος δρόμος ἀριστερά/δεξιά o prot-oss throm-oss areesteh-ra/ theksy*a*
Second left/right	Ὁ δεύτερος δρόμος ἀριστερά/δεξιά o thefteross throm-oss areesteh-ra/ theksy*a*
At the crossroads	Στό σταυροδρόμι sto stavro-thromee
At the traffic lights	Στά φανάρια sta fanar-ee-a
At the roundabout	Στή πλατεία stee plat-*ee*a
At the level-crossing	Στή διασταύρωση stee thee-astavro-see
It's near/far	Εἶναι κοντά/μακριά *ee*neh konda/makree-*a*
One kilometre	Ἕνα χιλιόμετρο enna heelee-ometro
Two kilometres	Δύο χιλιόμετρα thee-o heelee-ometra
Five minutes . . .	Πέντε λεπτά . . . pendeh lepta . . .
on foot	μέ τά πόδια meh ta poth-ya
by car	μέ τό αὐτοκίνητο meh toh aftok-*ee*neeto
Take . . .	Πᾶρτε . . . parteh . . .
the bus	τό λεωφορεῖο toh leh-of-oree-o
the ferry-boat	τό φέρυ μπώτ toh ferry-boat
the train	τό τραῖνο toh tren-o
the trolley-bus	τό τρόλλεϋ toh troll-ee
the underground	τόν ἠλεκτρικό ton eelektreek-o

[*For public transport, see p. 110*]

The tourist information office

ESSENTIAL INFORMATION

- Almost all towns in Greece have a tourist information office. Most towns have a Tourist Police, who control prices, inspect facilities and assist tourists generally. All road border control posts have an information desk.
- Look out for these words:
  ΓΡΑΦΕΙΟ ΕΛΛΗΝΙΚΟΥ ΟΡΓΑΝΙΣΜΟΥ ΤΟΥΡΙΣΜΟΥ (Greek Tourist Organization – EOT)
  ΤΟΥΡΙΣΤΙΚΗ ΑΣΤΥΝΟΜΙΑ (Tourist Police)
- These offices give you free information in the form of printed leaflets, foldouts, brochures, lists and plans.
- You may have to pay for some types of document.
- For finding a tourist office, see p. 22

WHAT TO SAY

Please have you got . . .	Παρακαλῶ, ἔχετε . . .
	parakalo eh-het-eh . . .
a plan of the town?	ἕνα χάρτη τῆς πόλης;
	enna hartee teess pol-eess
a list of hotels?	μία λίστα μέ ξενοδοχεῖα;
	mee-a leesta meh ksen-otho-hee-a
a list of campsites?	μία λίστα μέ κατασκηνώσεις;
	mee-a leesta meh kataskeen-osseess
a list of restaurants?	μία λίστα μέ ἐστιατόρια;
	mee-a leesta meh estee-atoria
a list of coach excursions?	μία λίστα μέ ἐκδρομές μέ πούλμαν;
	mee-a leesta meh ek-throm-ess meh poolman
a list of events?	μία λίστα μέ ἐκδηλώσεις;
	mee-a leesta meh ek-thee-losseess
a leaflet on the town?	ἕνα φυλλάδιο γιά τήν πόλη;
	enna feellath-yo ya teen pol-ee
a leaflet on the region?	ἕνα φυλλάδιο γιά τήν περιοχή;
	enna feellath-yo ya teen peri-ohee

Please have you got . . .	Παρακαλῶ, ἔχετε . . .
	parakalo eh-het-eh . . .
a railway timetable?	τά δρομολόγια γιά τά τραῖνα;
	ta thromolo-ya ya ta tren-a
a bus timetable?	τά δρομολόγια γιά τά λεωφορεῖα;
	ta thromolo-ya ya ta leh-of-oree-a
In English, please	Στ' Ἀγγλικά, σᾶς παρακαλῶ
	stangleeka sas parakalo
How much do I owe you?	Πόσο σᾶς ὀφείλω;
	posso sas ofeelo
Can you recommend . . .	Μπορεῖτε νά μοῦ προτείνετε . . .
	boreeteh na moo proteenet-eh . . .
a cheap hotel?	ἕνα φθηνό ξενοδοχεῖο;
	enna ftheeno ksen-otho-hee-o
a cheap restaurant?	ἕνα φθηνό ἑστιατόριο;
	enna ftheeno es-tee-atorio
Can you book a room/a table for me?	Μπορεῖτε νά μοῦ κλείσετε ἕνα δωμάτιο/ἕνα τραπέζι;
	boreeteh na moo kleesset-eh enna thomat-yo/enna trap-ez-ee

LIKELY ANSWERS

You need to understand when the answer is 'No'. You should be able to tell by the assistant's facial expression, tone of voice and gesture; but there are some language clues, such as:

No	Ὄχι
	o-hee
I'm sorry	Λυπᾶμαι
	leepam-eh
I don't have a list of campsites	Δέν ἔχω λίστα μέ κατασκηνώσεις
	then eh-ho leesta meh kataskeen-osseess
I haven't got any left	Δέν ἔχω ἄλλες
	then eh-ho alless
It's free	Εἶναι τσάμπα
	eeneh tsa-ba

Accommodation

Hotel

ESSENTIAL INFORMATION

- If you want hotel-type accommodation, all the following words in capital letters are worth looking for on name boards:
  ΞΕΝΟΔΟΧΕΙΟ (hotel)
  ΜΟΤΕΛ (motel)
  ΕΝΟΙΚΙΑΖΟΝΤΑΙ ΔΩΜΑΤΙΑ (rooms to let)
  ΞΕΝΙΑ (luxurious hotels and usually more expensive than ordinary hotels)
- A list of hotels in the town or district can usually be obtained at the local tourist office or at the local Tourist Police or police station. These lists are also available from the National Tourist Organization of Greece [see p. 7].
- Recommended hotels are classified into six categories: De luxe or AA and 1st to 5th class or A to E.
- The cost is displayed in the room itself; so you can check it when having a look around before agreeing to stay.
- The displayed cost is for the room itself, per night and not per person. Breakfast is extra and therefore optional.
- In small hotels and village rooms breakfast is paid for separately, if available.
- A Greek breakfast will usually consist of a cup of coffee or tea with bread, butter and jam or honey.
- A service charge of 15% is usually included in the bill but tipping is optional.
- Your passport is requested when registering at a hotel and will normally be kept overnight.
- Finding a hotel, see, p. 22.

WHAT TO SAY

I have a booking	Ἔχω κλείσει ἕνα δωμάτιο
	eh-ho kleessee enna thomat-yo
Have you any vacancies, please?	Ἔχετε δωμάτια, παρακαλῶ;
	eh-het-eh thomat-ya parakalo
Can I book a room?	Μπορῶ νά κλείσω ἕνα δωμάτιο;
	boro na kleeso enna thomat-yo

It's for . . .

Εἶναι γιά . . .
eeneh ya . . .

  one person

ἕνα ἄτομο
enna atomo

  two people

δύο ἄτομα
thee-o atoma

[*For numbers, see p. 125*]

It's for . . .

Εἶναι γιά . . .
eeneh ya . . .

  one night

μία βραδιά
mee-a vrath-ya

  two nights

δύο βραδιές
thee-o vrath-yes

  one week

μία βδομάδα
mee-a vthoma-tha

  two weeks

δύο βδομάδες
thee-o vthomath-ess

I would like . . .

Θά ἤθελα . . .
tha eethella . . .

  a (quiet) room

ἕνα (ἥσυχο) δωμάτιο
enna (eessee-ho) thomat-yo

  two rooms

δύο δωμάτια
thee-o thomat-ya

    with a single bed

μέ ἕνα μονό κρεββάτι
meh enna mono krevvat-ee

    with two single beds

μέ δύο μονά κρεββάτια
meh thee-o mona krevvat-ya

    with a double bed

μέ ἕνα διπλό κρεββάτι
meh enna theeplo krevvat-ee

    with a toilet

μέ τουαλέτα
meh too-al-eh-ta

    with a bathroom

μέ μπάνιο
meh ban-yo

    with a shower

μέ ντούς
meh dooss

    with a cot

μέ παιδικό κρεββάτι
meh peh-theeko krevvat-ee

    with a balcony

μέ μπαλκόνι
meh balkon-ee

Do you serve meals?

Σερβίρετε γεύματα;
sehrveer-et-eh gevmata

At what time is ...	Τί ὥρα σερβίρετε ... tee ora serv-eer-et-eh ...
breakfast?	τό πρωινό; toh pro-eeno
lunch?	τό γεῦμα; toh gevma
dinner?	τό δεῖπνο; toh theepno
How much is it?	Πόσο κάνει; posso kanee
Can I look at the room?	Μπορῶ νά δῶ τό δωμάτιο; boro na tho toh thomat-yo
I'd prefer a room ...	Θά προτιμοῦσα ἕνα δωμάτιο ... tha proteem-oossa enna thomat-yo ...
at the front/at the back	μπροστά/πίσω brosta/peesso
OK, I'll take it	Ἐντάξει, θά τό πάρω endaksee tha toh par-o
No thanks, I won't take it	Ὄχι εὐχαριστῶ, δέν θά τό πάρω o-hee ef-har-eesto then tha toh par-o
The key to number (10), please	Τό κλειδί γιά τό νούμερο (δέκα), παρακαλῶ toh kleethee ya toh noomero (thek-a) parakalo
Please, may I have ...	Νά μοῦ δώσετε ... na moo thoh-set-eh ...
a coat hanger?	μία κρεμάστρα; mee-a kreh-mastra
a towel?	μία πετσέτα; mee-a petset-a
a glass?	ἕνα ποτήρι; enna pot-eeree
some soap?	ἕνα σαπούνι; enna sapoonee
an ashtray?	ἕνα τασάκι; enna tasahkee
another pillow?	ἄλλο ἕνα μαξιλάρι; allo enna maks-eelaree
another blanket?	ἄλλη μία κουβέρτα; allee mee-a koo-vehr-ta

Come in!	Περάστε! peh-*ra*steh
One moment, please!	Ἕνα λεπτό, σᾶς παρακαλῶ! *e*nna lept*o* sas parakal*o*
Please can you . . .	Μπορεῖτε παρακαλῶ νά . . . bor*ee*teh parakal*o* na . . .
do this laundry/dry cleaning?	πλύνετε αὐτό στό πλυντήριο/ στεγνοκαθαριστήριο; pl*ee*net-eh aft*o* sto pleend*ee*rio/ stegno-kathar-eest*ee*rio
call me at . . .?	μέ τηλεφωνήσετε στίς . . .; meh teelef-on-*ee*sset-eh steess . . .
help me with my luggage?	μέ βοηθήσετε μέ τά πράγματα; meh vo-eeth-*ee*sset-eh meh ta pr*a*gmatah
call me a taxi for . . .?	καλέσετε ἕνα ταξί γιά . . .; kal-*e*sset-eh *e*nna taks*ee* ya . . .

[*For times, see p. 127*]

The bill, please	Τό λογαριασμό, παρακαλῶ toh logaree-azm*o* parakal*o*
Is service included?	Εἶναι μέ τό σερβίς; *ee*neh meh toh serv*ee*ss
I think this is wrong	Νομίζω πώς αὐτό εἶναι λάθος nom-*ee*zo poss aft*o* *ee*neh l*a*th-oss
May I have a receipt?	Μπορῶ νά ἔχω μία ἀπόδειξη; bor*o* na *e*hho m*ee*-a apoth-*ee*ksee

At breakfast

Some more . . . please	Καί ἄλλο . . . παρακαλῶ keh *a*llo . . . parakal*o*
coffee	καφέ kaf-*eh*
tea	τσάϊ ts*a*-ee
bread	ψωμί psom-*ee*
butter	βούτυρο v*oo*teero
honey	μέλι

Some more jam	Καί ἄλλη μαρμελάδα
	keh allee marmelatha
May I have a boiled egg?	Νά πάρω ἕνα βραστό αὐγό;
	nah paro enna vrasto avgo

LIKELY REACTIONS

Have you an identity document, please?	Ἔχετε ταυτότητα, παρακαλῶ;
	eh-het-eh taftot-eeta parakalo
What's your name?	Πῶς λέγεσται;
	poss legesteh
Sorry, we're full	Λυπᾶμαι, δέν ἔχουμε δωμάτιο
	leepam-eh then eh-hoomeh thomat-yo
I haven't any rooms left	Δέν ἔχουμε δωμάτια
	then eh-hoomeh thomat-ya
Do you want to have a look?	Θέλετε νά ρίξετε μία ματιά;
	thel-et-eh na reekset-eh mee-a mat-ya
How many people is it for?	Γιά πόσα ἄτομα εἶναι;
	ya possa atoma een-eh
We only serve breakfast	Σερβίρουμε πρωινό μόνο
	serv-eer-oom-eh pro-een-o mon-o
From (seven o'clock) onwards	Μετά τίς (ἑπτά)
	met-a teess (epta)
From (midday) onwards	Μετά τίς (δώδεκα)
	met-a teess (thoth-eka)

[For times, see p. 127]

It's (200) drachmas	(διακόσες) δραχμές
	(thee-akoss-ess) thra-hmess

[For numbers, see p. 125]

Camping and youth hostelling

ESSENTIAL INFORMATION

Camping

● Look for the word: KAMΠINΓK (camping) or this sign.
Note μ = metres.

● Be prepared for the following charges:
per person
for the car (if applicable)
for the tent or caravan plot
for electricity
for hot showers
● A reduction of 10% is made to the holders of AIT or FIA membership cards.
● You must provide proof of identity, such as your passport.
● Passports or identity cards can be returned to their holders only on settlement of the account.
● For the NTOG camping sites, which are better organized, advanced booking is strongly recommended.
● Camping is tolerated almost anywhere outside built-up areas but it is always best to get the landowner's permission beforehand. The police have the right to forbid you camping off-site in case of overcrowding, poor hygiene etc.

Youth hostels

● Look for the word: ΞΕΝΩΝ ΝΕΟΤΗΤΟΣ (youth hostel) or the sign shown on the next page.

- The charge per night is the same everywhere.
- You must have a YHA card.
- Accommodation is in dormitories.
- In most youth hostels there are cafeterias where light meals and drinks can be bought at reasonable prices.
- For finding a campsite and youth hostel, see p. 22.
- For buying or replacing camping equipment, see p. 56.

WHAT TO SAY

I have a booking	Ἔχω κρατήσει θέση
	eh-ho krateé-see thessee
Have you any vacancies?	Ἔχετε θέσεις;
	eh-het-eh thesseess
It's for . . .	Εἶναι γιά . . .
	eeneh ya . . .
one adult/one person	ἕναν ἐνήλικο/ἕνα ἄτομο
	ennan en-eeleeko/enna atomo
two adults/two people	δύο ἐνήλικες/δύο ἄτομα
	thee-o en-eeleekess/thee-o atoma
and one child	καί ἕνα παιδί
	keh enna peth-ee
and two children	καί δύο παιδιά
	keh theeo peth-ya
It's for . . .	Εἶναι γιά . . .
	eeneh ya . . .
one night	μία βραδιά
	mee-a vrath-ya
two nights	δύο βραδιές
	thee-o vrath-yes
one week	μία βδομάδα
	mee-a vthoma-tha
two weeks	δύο βδομάδες
	thee-o vthomath-ess

How much is it . . .	Πόσο κάνει . . . posso kan-ee . . .
for the tent?	ἡ σκηνή; ee skeenee
for the caravan?	τό κάραβαν; toh karavan
for the car?	τό αὐτοκίνητο; toh aftokeen-eeto
for the electricity?	τό ἡλεκτρικό; toh eelek-treeko
per person?	τό ἄτομο; toh atomo
per day/night?	τή μέρα/βραδιά; tee meh-ra/vrath-ya
May I look round?	Μπορῶ νά ρίξω μιά ματιά; boro na reekso mee-a mat-ya
Do you close the gate at night?	Κλειδώνετε τήν πόρτα τή νύκτα; kleethon-et-eh teen porta tee neehta
Do you provide anything . . .	Σερβίρετε . . . sehr-veer-et-eh . . .
to eat?	φαγητό; fag-eeto
to drink?	ποτά; pota
Is there/are there . . .	Ἔχετε . . . eh-het-eh . . .
a bar	μπάρ; bar
hot showers?	ζεστά ντούς; zesta dooss
a kitchen?	κουζίνα; koozeena
a laundry?	πλυντήριο; pleendeerio
a restaurant?	ἑστιατόριο; estee-atorio
a shop?	μαγαζί; magaz-ee
a swimming pool?	πισίνα; peeseena

[*For food shopping, see p. 63, and for eating and drinking out, see p. 79*]

Where are . . .	Πού εἶναι . . .
	poo eeneh . . .
the dustbins?	οἱ σκουπιδοτενεκέδες;
	ee skoo-peethoten-ek-eth-ess
the showers?	τά ντούς;
	ta dooss
the toilets?	οἱ τουαλέτες;
	ee too-al-et-ess
At what time must one . . .	Τί ὥρα πρέπει . . .
	tee ora prehpee . . .
go to bed?	νά κοιμηθοῦμε;
	na keemeethoom-eh
get up?	νά ξυπνήσουμε;
	na kseep-neessoom-eh
Please have you got . . .	Ἔχετε . . . παρακαλῶ
	eh-het-eh . . . parakalo
a broom?	μία σκούπα;
	mee-a skoopa
a corkscrew?	ἕνα ἀνοικτήρι;
	enna an-eekteeree
a drying-up cloth?	μία πετσέτα γιά τά πιάτα;
	mee-a petset-a ya ta pee-at-a
a fork?	ἕνα πηρούνι;
	enna pee-roonee
a fridge?	ψυγεῖο;
	pseeg-ee-o
a frying pan?	ἕνα τηγάνι;
	enna teegan-ee
an iron?	ἕνα σίδερο;
	enna seethero
a knife?	ἕνα μαχαίρι;
	enna ma-he-ree
a plate?	ἕνα πιάτο;
	enna pee-at-o
a saucepan?	μία κατσαρόλα;
	mee-a katsarol-a
a teaspoon?	ἕνα κουταλάκι;
	enna koot-alak-ee
a tin opener?	ἕνα ἀνοικτήρι γιά κονσέρβες;
	enna aneek-teeree ya kon-sehr-vess
any washing powder?	σκόνη πλυσίματος;
	skon-ee pleess-eemat-oss
any washing-up liquid?	ὑγρό γιά τά πιάτα;
	eegro ya ta pee-at-a

The bill, please   Τό λογαριασμό, παρακαλῶ
                        toh logaree-azm*o* parakal*o*

Problems

The toilet   Ἡ τουαλέτα
                        ee too-al-*et*-a

The shower   Τό ντούς
                        toh d*oo*ss

The tap   Ἡ βρύση
                        ee vr*ee*ssee

The razor point   Ἡ πρίζα γιά τή ξυριστική
                               μηχανή
                        ee pr*ee*za ya tee kseer-eest*eek-ee*
                        mee-han-*ee*

The light   Τό φῶς
                        toh f*o*ss

. . . is not working   . . . χάλασε
                        . . . h*a*l-ass-*eh*

My camping gas has run out   Ἡ φιάλη ὑγραερίου τελείωσε
                        ee fee-*a*l-ee eegra-ehr-*ee*-oo
                        tel*ee*-osseh

The bill, please   Τό λογαριασμό, παρακαλῶ
                        toh logaree-azm*o* parakal*o*

LIKELY REACTIONS

Have you an identity document?	Ἔχετε ταυτότητα; eh-het-eh taftot-eeta
Your membership card, please	Τήν κάρτα σας, παρακαλῶ teen karta sas parakalo
What's your name?	Πῶς ὀνομάζεστε; poss on-omaz-es-teh
Sorry, we're full	Λυπᾶμαι, ἀλλά δέν ἔχουμε θέση leepam-eh alla then ehoomeh thessee
How many people is it for?	Γιά πόσα ἄτομα εἶναι; ya possa atoma eeneh
How many nights is it for?	Γιά πόσες βραδιές εἶναι; ya possess vrath-yes eeneh
It's (80) drachmas ...	(Ὀγδόντα) δραχμές ... (ogthonda) thra-hmess ...
per day/per night	τή μέρα/τή βραδιά tee meh-ra/tee vrath-ya

Rented accommodation: problem solving

ESSENTIAL INFORMATION

- If you're looking for accommodation to rent, look out for:
  ΕΝΟΙΚΙΑΖΕΤΑΙ (for rent)
  ΔΙΑΜΕΡΙΣΜΑΤΑ (apartments)
  ΔΩΜΑΤΙΑ (rooms)
  ΜΠΑΓΚΑΛΟΟΤΣ (bungalows)
- For arranging details of your let, see 'Hotel' p. 29.
- Key words you will meet if renting on the spot:
  μία προκαταβολή   deposit
  mee-a pro-katavol-*ee*
  τό κλειδί   key
  toh kleeth*ee*

- Having arranged your own accommodation and arrived with the key, check the obvious basics that you take for granted at home.
  Electricity: Voltage? Razors and small appliances brought from home may need adjusting. You may need an adaptor.
  Gas: Outside Athens, there is only bottled gas, and this is always butane gas.
  Stove: Don't be surprised to find:
  —the grill inside the oven, or no grill at all
  —a lid covering the rings which lifts up to form a 'splash-back'
  Toilet: Don't flush disposable diapers or anything else down the toilet, since the pipes are narrow and block easily. A bin is always provided.
  Water: Find the stopcock. Check taps and plugs — they may not operate in the way you are used to. Check how to turn on (or light) the hot water.
  Windows: Check the method of opening and closing windows and shutters.
  Insects: Is an insecticide spray provided? If not, get one locally.
  Equipment: See p. 56 for buying or replacing equipment.
- You will probably have an official agent, but be clear in your own mind who to contact in an emergency, even if it is only a neighbour in the first place.

WHAT TO SAY

My name is . . .	Ὀνομάζομαι . . .
	on-omaz-om-eh . . .
I'm staying at . . .	Μένω στό . . .
	men-o sto . . .
They've cut off . . .	Ἔκοψαν . . .
	ek-opsan . . .
the electricity	τό ἠλεκτρικό
	toh eelek-treeko
the gas	τό γκάζι
	toh gazee
the water	τό νερό
	toh neh-ro
Is there . . . in the area?	Ὑπάρχει . . . στή περιοχή
	eepar-hee . . . stee peri-ohee
an electrician	ἠλεκτρολόγος;
	eelektro-log-oss
a plumber	ὑδραυλικός;
	eethrav-leekoss
Where is . . .	Ποῦ εἶναι . . .
	poo eeneh . . .
the fuse box?	ἡ ἀσφάλεια;
	ee asfal-ya
the stopcock?	ὁ διακόπτης τοῦ νεροῦ;
	o thee-ak-opteess too nehr-oo
the water heater?	τό θερμοσίφωνο;
	toh thermoss-eefon-o
Is there central heating?	Ὑπάρχει καλοριφέρ;
	eepar-hee kaloreefer
The cooker	Ἡ κουζίνα
	ee koozeena
The hair dryer	Τό σεσουάρ
	toh seh-soo-ar
The heating	Ἡ θέρμανση
	ee thehr-man-see
The immersion heater	Τό θερμοσίφωνο
	toh thermo-seefon-o
The iron	Τό σίδερο
	toh seethero
The refrigerator	Τό ψυγείο
	toh pseeg-ee-o

The telephone	Τό τηλέφωνο
	Toh teelef-on-o
The toilet	Ἡ τουαλέτα
	ee too-al-et-a
The washing machine	Τό πλυντήριο
	toh pleendeerio
... is not working	... χάλασε
	... hal-ass-eh
Where can I get ...	Ποῦ μπορῶ νά βρῶ ...
	poo boro na vro ...
an adaptor for this?	ἕνα μετασχηματιστή γιά αὐτό;
	enna met-ass-hee-mat-ees-tee ya afto
a bottle of gas?	μία φιάλη γκάζι;
	mee-a fee-al-ee gazee
a fuse?	μία ἀσφάλεια;
	mee-a asfalya
an insecticide spray?	ἕνα ἐντομοκτόνο;
	enna endomokton-o
a light bulb	μία λάμπα;
	mee-a lamba
The drain	Ἡ ἀποχέτευση
	ee apo-het-ef-see
The sink	Ὁ νεροχύτης
	o nehro-heeteess
The toilet	Ἡ τουαλέτα
	ee too-al-et-a
... is blocked	... βούλωσε
	... vooloss-eh
The gas is leaking	Ὑπάρχει διαρροή γκάζι
	eepar-hee thee-arro-ee gazee
Can you mend it straightaway?	Μπορεῖτε νά τό ἐπισκευάσετε ἀμέσως;
	boreeteh na toh ep-eeskev-asset-eh a-mes-oss
When can you mend it?	Πότε θά τό ἐπισκευάσετε;
	pot-eh tha toh ep-eeskev-asset-eh
How much do I owe you?	Πόσο σᾶς ὀφείλω;
	posso sas ofeelo
When is the rubbish collected?	Πότε περνάει ὁ σκουπιδιάρης;
	pot-eh pehr-na-ee o skoopeeth-yar-eess

LIKELY REACTIONS

What's your name?	Πῶς λέγεσται; poss legesteh
What's your address?	Ποία εἶναι ἡ διεύθυνση σας; pee-a eeneh ee thee-ef-theen-see sas
There's a shop . . .	Ὑπάρχει μαγαζί . . . eeparhee magaz-ee . . .
in town	στήν πόλη steen pol-ee
in the village	στό χωριό sto horee-o
I can't come . . .	Δέν μπορῶ νά ἔρθω . . . then boro na ehr-tho . . .
today	σήμερα seemera
this week	αὐτή τή βδομάδα aftee tee vthoma-tha
until Monday	πρίν τή Δευτέρα preen tee thef-tehra
I can come . . .	Μπορῶ νά ἔρθω . . . boro na ehr-tho . . .
on Tuesday	τή Τρίτη tee treetee
when you want	ὅποτε θέλετε op-ot-eh thel-et-eh
Every day	Κάθε μέρα kath-eh mehra
Every other day	Μέρα παρά μέρα mehra para mehra
On (Wednesdays)	Κάθε (Τετάρτη) kath-eh (tet-artee)

[For days of the week, see p. 129]

General shopping

The drug store/The chemist's

ESSENTIAL INFORMATION

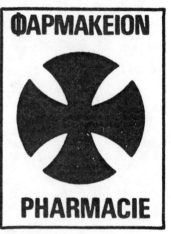

- Look for the word
  ΦAPMAKEION (drug store)
  or this sign.
- Medicines (drugs) are only
  available at a drug store.
  Some non-drugs can be bought
  at a supermarket or
  department store, of course.
- Try the drug store *before* going
  to a doctor: they are usually
  qualified to treat minor
  injuries.
- Drug stores take it in turns
  to stay open all night
  and on Sundays.
  A drug store will display an
  illuminated list of all-night
  drug stores (ΔIANYKTEPETONTA ΦAPMAKEIA).
- Normal opening times are: 8.00 a.m. to 1.00 p.m. and 5.30 p.m. to
  8.30 p.m. but you can check with the local tourist office.
- If you don't have insurance, you can be offered free medical service
  in certain state hospitals provided you can prove that you are
  uninsured and unable through personal financial means to cover the
  expenses of the medical treatment. However, this service is *extremely*
  limited and it is very unwise not to be properly insured.
- Some toiletries can also be bought at a
  KATAΣTHMA KAΛΛYNTIKΩN (perfumery).
- Finding a drug store, see p. 22.

WHAT TO SAY

I'd like . . .	Θά ἤθελα . . .
	tha *eethella* . . .
some Alka Seltzer	αλκασέλτζερ
	alka seltzer
some antiseptic	ἕνα ἀντισηπτικό
	enna antee-seepteek*o*
some aspirin	ἕνα κουτί ἀσπιρίνες
	enna kootee aspeer-*ee*ness
some bandage	ἕνα ἐπίδεσμο
	enna ep-*ee*thezm*o*
some cotton wool	ἕνα βαμβάκι
	enna vamvak-ee
some eye drops	σταγόνες γιά τά μάτια
	stagon-ess ya ta mat-ya
some foot powder	ποῦδρα γιά τά πόδια
	poothra ya ta poth-ya
some gauze dressing	μερικές γάζες
	mehr-eekess gaz-ess
some inhalant	κάτι γιά εἰσπνοές
	kat-ee ya eess-pno-*ess*
some insect repellent	ἕνα ἐντομοκτόνο
	enna endomokton-*o*
some lip salve	μία ἀλοιφή γιά τά χείλη
	mee-a al-eefee ya ta heelee
some nose drops	σταγόνες γιά τή μύτη
	stagon-ess ya tee meetee
some sticking plaster	ἕνα λευκοπλάστη
	enna lefkoplastee
some throat pastilles	παστίλλιες γιά τό λαιμό
	pasteel-ee-ess ya toh lem-*o*
some Vaseline	μία βαζελίνη
	mee-a vaz-el-*ee*nee
I'd like something for . . .	Θά ἤθελα κάτι γιά. . . .
	tha *eethella* kat-ee ya . . .
bites	τσίμπημα
	ts*ee*m-beema
burns	ἔγκαυμα
	*e*ngavma
chilblains	χιονίστρες
	hee-on-*ee*stress

I'd like something for . . .
Θά ἤθελα κάτι γιά . . .
tha *eethella* kat-ee ya . . .

a cold
ἕνα κρύωμα
enna kr*ee*oma

constipation
δυσκοιλιότητα
theeskeelee-*ot*-eeta

a cough
τόν βῆχα
ton vee-ha

diarrhoea
διάρροια
thee-*arria*

earache
πόνο στό αὐτί
pon-o sto aft*ee*

flu
γρίππη
gr*ee*pee

scalds
κάψιμο
kapseemo

sore gums
σπυράκια
speerak-ya

sprains
στραμπούλῃγμα
stram-*boo*leegma

stings
κεντρίσματα
ken-dreezmata

sunburn
ἔγκαυμα ἡλίου
engavma eel*ee*-oo

sea/travel sickness
ναυτία
naft*ee*-a

I need . . .
Χρειάζομαι . . .
hree*azomeh* . . .

some baby food
βρεφική τροφή
vrefeek*ee* trof-*ee*

some contraceptives
προφυλακτικά
prof-eelak-teek*a*

some deodorant
ἕνα ἀποσμητικό
enna ap-ozmee-teek*o*

some disposable nappies
πάνες μίας χρήσεως
pan-ess m*ee*-ass hreess-eh-oss

some handcream
μία κρέμα γιά τά χέρια
m*ee*-a krem-a ya ta hehria

some lipstick
ἕνα κραγιόν
enna kra-yon

some make-up remover	βαμβάκι γιά τόν καθαρισμό τοῦ προσώπου
	vamvak-ee ya ton kathar-eezmo too prossop-oo
some paper tissues	χαρτομάνδηλα
	hart-oman-theela
some razor blades	ξυραφάκια
	kseer-afak-ya
some safety pins	παραμάνες
	paraman-ess
some sanitary towels	σερβιέτες ὑγείας
	sehr-vee-et-ess eeg-ee-ass
some shaving cream	μία ξυριστική κρέμα
	mee-a kseer-eesteek-ee krem-a
some soap	ἕνα σαπούνι
	enna sap-oonee
some suntan lotion/oil	μία ἀντιηλιακή κρέμα/λάδι
	mee-a antee-eelee-ak-ee krem-a/lathee
some talcum powder	ἕνα τάλκ
	enna talc
some Tampax	ἕνα ταμπάξ
	enna tampax
some toilet paper	ἕνα χαρτί ὑγείας
	enna hartee ee-yee-ass
some toothpaste	μία ὀδοντόκρεμα
	mee-a othond-okrem-a

[*For other essential expressions, see 'Shop talk', p. 58*]

Holiday items

ESSENTIAL INFORMATION

- Places to shop at and signs to look for:
  ΒΙΒΛΙΟΠΩΛΕΙΟ (bookshop)
  ΧΑΡΤΟΠΩΛΕΙΟ (stationery)
  ΦΩΤΟΓΡΑΦΙΚΑ ΕΙΔΗ (photographic items)
- and the main department stores:
  MARINOPOULOS
  MINION
  ATHENÈE
  TSITSOPOULOS
- The pavement kiosks (ΠΕΡΙΠΤΕΡΑ) are particularly useful as they are open late at night and sell a variety of goods such as aspirins, razor blades, playing cards, pens, soft drinks, etc. See also 'The smoke shop' p. 50 and 'Telephoning' p. 100.

WHAT TO SAY

Where can I buy . . . ?	Πού μπορῶ ν'ἀγοράσω . . .;
	poo boro nag-ora-so . . .
I'd like . . .	Θά ἤθελα . . .
	tha eethella . . .
a bag	μία τσάντα
	mee-a tsanda
a beach ball	μία μπάλλα
	mee-a balla
a bucket	ἕνα κουβᾶ
	enna koova
an English newspaper	μία ἀγγλική ἐφημερίδα
	mee-a ang-leekee ef-eemehr-eetha
some envelopes	μερικούς φακέλους
	mehr-eek-ooss fak-el-ooss
a guide book	ἕνα βιβλίο ὁδηγό
	enna veev-lee-o othee-go
a map (of the area)	ἕνα χάρτη (τῆς περιοχῆς)
	enna hartee (teess peri-oheess)
some postcards	μερικές κάρτες
	mehr-eek-ess kartess

a spade	ἕνα φτυάρι
	enna ftee-*ar*-ee
a straw hat	ἕνα ψάθινο καπέλλο
	enna psathee-no kapello
a suitcase	μία βαλίτσα
	mee-a valeet-sa
some sunglasses	γυαλιά ἡλίου
	yal-ya eelee-oo
a sunshade	μία τέντα ἡλίου
	mee-a tenda eelee-oo
an umbrella	μία ὀμπρέλλα
	mee-a ombrella
some writing paper	χαρτί ἀλληλογραφίας
	hartee alleel-ograf-*ee*-ass
I'd like . . . *[show the camera]*	Θά ἤθελα . . .
	tha *ee*thella . . .
a colour film	ἕνα ἔγχρωμο φίλμ
	enna en-hrom-o film
a black and white film	ἕνα ἀσπρόμαυρο φίλμ
	enna assprom-avro film
for prints	γιά φωτογραφίες
	ya fotograf-*ee*-ess
for slides	γιά σλάϊτς
	ya slides
12(24/36) exposures	γιά δώδεκα (εἴκοσι-τέσσερες/ τριάντα-ἔξη) φωτογραφίες
	ya thothe-ka (eekossee tesser-ess/ tree-anda eksee) fotograf-*ee*-ess
a standard 8 mm film	ἕνα κανονικό φίλμ τῶν ὀκτώ μιλιμέτρ
	enna kan-on-eeko-o film ton okto millimetr
a super 8 film	ἕνα φίλμ σοῦπερ ὀκτώ
	enna film sooper okto
some flash bulbs	μερικά φλάς
	mehr-eeka flass
This camera is broken	Αὐτή ἡ φωτογραφική μηχανή χάλασε
	aftee ee fotografeekee meehanee halass-eh
The film is stuck	Τό φίλμ ἔχει μπλεχτεῖ
	toh film ehee bleh-htee

Please can you . . . Παρακαλῶ μπορεῖτε νά . . .
parakalo boreeteh na . . .

develop/print this? ἐμφανίσετε/ἐκτυπώσετε αὐτό;
emfan-eesset-eh/ek-teeposset-eh afto

load the camera for me? βάλετε τό φίλμ μέσα;
valet-eh toh film messa

[*For other essential expressions, see 'Shop talk', p. 58*]

The smoke shop

ESSENTIAL INFORMATION

- Tobacco is sold mainly in pavement kiosks called ΠΕΡΙΠΤΕΡΑ.
- To ask if there is one nearby, see p. 22.
- Kiosks always sell newspapers (Greek and foreign), sweets and sometimes postage stamps. See also p. 48 and p. 100.

WHAT TO SAY

A packet of cigarettes . . . Ἕνα πακέτο τσιγάρα . . .
enna pak-et-o tseegara . . .

with filters μέ φίλτρο
meh feeltro

without filters χωρίς φίλτρο
horeess feeltro

menthol μέντας
men-tass

Those up there . . . Ἐκεῖνα ἐκεῖ πάνω . . .
ek-eena ek-ee pan-o . . .

on the right δεξιά
theks-ya

on the left ἀριστερά
areesteh-ra

These [*point*] Αὐτά
afta

Cigarettes, please . . . Τσιγάρα, παρακαλῶ . . .
tseegara parakalo . . .

100, 200, 300 ἑκατό, διακόσια, τριακόσια
ek-at-o, thee-akoss-ya,
tree-akoss-ya

Two packets	δύο πακέτα
	th*ee*-o pak-et-a
Have you got . . .	Ἔχετε . . .
	eh-het-eh . . .
English cigarettes?	ἐγγλέζικα τσιγάρα;
	englez-eeka tseeg*a*ra
American cigarettes?	ἀμερικάνικα τσιγάρα;
	amerikan-eeka tseeg*a*ra
English pipe tobacco?	ἐγγλέζικο καπνό γιά πίπα;
	englez-eeko kapn-o ya p*ee*pa
American pipe tobacco?	ἀμερικάνικο καπνό γιά πίπα;
	amerikan-eek-o kapno ya p*ee*pa
A packet of pipe tobacco	Ἕνα πακέτο μέ καπνό πίπας
	enna paket-o meh kapno p*ee*p-ass
That one up there . . .	Ἐκεῖνο ἐκεῖ πάνω . . .
	ek-*ee*no ek-ee pan-o . . .
on the right	δεξιά
	theks-y*a*
on the left	ἀριστερά
	areesteh-r*a*
This one [*point*]	Αὐτό
	aft*o*
A cigar, please	Ἕνα ποῦρο, παρακαλῶ
	enna p*oo*-ro parakal*o*
(Some) cigars	Ποῦρα
	p*oo*-ra
Those [*point*]	Ἐκεῖνα
	ek-*ee*na
A box of matches	Σπίρτα
	sp*ee*rta
A packet of pipe cleaners	Ἕνα πακέτο μέ καθαριστές πίπας
	enna pak-et-o meh kathar-eestess p*ee*p-ass
A packet of flints	Ἕνα πακέτο μέ πέτρες
[*Show lighter*]	enna pak-et-o meh petress
Lighter fuel	Βενζίνη γιά ἀναπτῆρα παρακαλῶ
	venzeenee ya anapteera parakal*o*
Lighter gas, please	Ἀέριο γιά ἀναπτῆρα
	a-ehrio ya anapt*ee*ra

[*For other essential expressions, see 'Shop talk', p. 58*)

Buying clothes

ESSENTIAL INFORMATION

- Look for:
  ΓΥΝΑΙΚΕΙΑ ΕΝΔΥΜΑΤΑ (women's clothes)
  ΑΝΔΡΙΚΑ ΕΝΔΥΜΑΤΑ (men's clothes)
  ΥΠΟΔΗΜΑΤΟΠΟΙΕΙΟΝ (shoe shop)
- Don't buy without being measured first or without trying things on.
- Don't rely on conversion charts of clothing sizes (see p. 139).
- If you are buying for someone else, take their measurements with you.

WHAT TO SAY

I'd like . . .	Θά ἤθελα . . .
	tha eethella . . .
an anorak	ἕνα ἀνοράκ
	enna anorak
a belt	μία ζώνη
	mee-a zon-ee
a bikini	ἕνα μπικίνι
	enna bikini
a bra	ἕνα σουτιέν
	enna sootyen
a cap (swimming, skiing)	ἕνα σκοῦφο (γιά τή θάλασσα/γιά σκί)
	enna skoofo (ya tee thal-assa/ya skee)
a cardigan	μία ζακέτα
	mee-a zak-et-a
a coat	ἕνα παλτό
	enna palto
a dress	ἕνα φόρεμα
	enna for-ema
a hat	ἕνα καπέλλο
	enna kapello
a jacket	Ἕνα σακκάκι
	enna sakkak-ee
a jumper	μία μπλούζα
	mee-a blooza

a nightdress	ἕνα νυχτικό
	enna nee-hteeko
a pullover	ἕνα πουλόβερ
	enna pool-ovehr
a raincoat	ἕνα ἀδιάβροχο
	enna athee-avro-ho
a shirt	ἕνα πουκάμισο
	enna pookam-eeso
a skirt	μία φούστα
	mee-a foosta
a suit	ἕνα κοστούμι
	enna kostoomee
a swimsuit	ἕνα μαγιό
	enna ma-yo
a T-shirt	ἕνα μπλουζάκι
	enna bloozak-ee
I'd like a pair of . . .	Θά ἤθελα . . .
	tha eethella . . .
briefs (women)	μία κυλλότα
	mee-a keelot-a
gloves	γάντια
	gandia
jeans	ἕνα μπλού-τζήν
	enna blue-jean
pyjamas	μία πυτζάμα
	mee-a peetza-ma
shorts	ἕνα σόρτ
	enna sort
socks	κάλτσες ἀνδρικές
	kalt-sess andreek-ess
stockings	κάλτσες γυναικείες
	kalt-sess gheenek-ee-ess
tights	ἕνα καλσόν
	enna kalson
trousers	ἕνα πανταλόνι
	enna pantal-on-ee
underpants (men)	ἕνα σλίπ
	enna slip
I'd like a pair of . . .	Θά ἤθελα . . .
	tha eethella . . .
shoes	παπούτσια
	papootsia
canvas shoes	ἐλβιέλες
	elvee-el-ess

I'd like a pair of . . . Θά ἤθελα . . .
   tha eethella . . .

   sandals πέδιλα
      peth-eela

   beach shoes σανδάλια
      san-thal-ya

   smart shoes βραδυνά παπούτσια
      vrathee-na papoots-ia

   boots μπότες
      bot-ess

   moccasins μοκασίνια
      mokas-eenya

My size is . . . Τό νούμερο μου εἶναι . . .
[For numbers, see p. 125] toh noomero moo eeneh

Can you measure me, please? Μπορεῖτε νά μοῦ πάρετε τά μέτρα,
      παρακαλῶ;
      boreeteh na moo par-et-eh ta metra
      parakalo

Can I try it on? Μπορῶ νά τό δοκιμάσω;
   boro na toh thok-eema-so

It's for a present Εἶναι γιά δῶρο
   eeneh ya thoro

These are the measurements Αὐτά εἶναι τά μέτρα
[show written] afta eeneh ta metra

   bust στῆθος
      steethoss

   chest στῆθος
      steeth-oss

   collar κολλάρο
      kollar-o

   hip περιφέρεια
      peri-fehria

   leg πόδι
      poth-ee

   waist μέση
      messe

Have you got something . . . Ἔχετε κάτι . . .
   eh-het-eh kat-ee . . .

   in black? σέ μαῦρο;
      seh mavro

   in white? σέ ἄσπρο;
      seh aspro

in grey?	σέ γκρί; seh gree
in blue?	σέ μπλέ; seh bleh
in brown?	σέ καφέ; seh kafeh
in pink?	σέ ρόζ; seh roz
in green?	σέ πράσινο; seh pras-eeno
in red?	σέ κόκκινο; seh kok-eeno
in yellow?	σέ κίτρινο; seh keetreeno
in this colour? [point]	σέ αὐτό τό χρῶμα; seh afto toh hroma
in cotton?	σέ βαμβακερό; seh vamvak-ehro
in denim?	σέ τραχύ ὕφασμα; seh trahee eefazma
in leather?	σέ δέρμα; seh thehr-ma
in nylon?	σέ νάϋλον; seh na-eelon
in suede?	σέ σουέτ; seh soo-et
in wool?	σέ μάλλινο; seh malleeno
in this material? [point]	σέ αὐτό τό ὕφασμα; seh afto toh eefazma

[For other essential expressions, see 'Shop talk', p. 58]

Replacing equipment

ESSENTIAL INFORMATION

- Look for these shops and signs:
  ΣΙΔΗΡΟΠΩΛΕΙΟΝ (hardware)
  ΗΛΕΚΤΡΙΚΑ ΕΙΔΗ (electrical goods)
  ΨΙΛΙΚΑ (household cleaning material)
- To ask the way to the shop, see p. 22.
- At a campsite try their shop first.

WHAT TO SAY

Have you got . . .	Έχετε . . .
	eh-het-eh . . .
an adaptor? [*show appliance*]	ἕνα μετασχηματιστή;
	enna met-ass-heema-teest-*ee*
a bottle of butane gas?	ἕνα μπουκάλι γκάζι;
	enna book*a*lee g*a*zee
a bottle opener?	ἀνοικτήρι γιά μπουκάλια;
	an-eekt*ee*ree ya book*a*lya
a corkscrew?	ἀνοικτήρι φιάλης;
	an-eekt*ee*ree fee-*a*l-eess
any disinfectant?	ἕνα ἀπολυμαντικό;
	enna apol-eemandeek*o*
any disposable cups?	χάρτινα φλυτζάνια;
	h*a*rteena fleet-z*a*n-ya
any disposable plates?	χάρτινα πιάτα;
	h*a*rteena pee-*a*t-a
a drying up cloth?	πανί γιά τά πιάτα;
	pan-*ee* ya ta pee-*a*t-a
any forks?	πηρούνια;
	peeroonia
a fuse? [*show old one*]	ἀσφάλεια;
	asf*a*l-ya
an insecticide spray?	ἕνα ἐντομοκτόνο;
	enna endomokton-*o*
a paper kitchen roll?	ἕνα ρολό γιά κουζίνα (χαρτί);
	enna rolo ya koozeena (hart*ee*)
any knives?	μαχαίρια;
	ma-hehrya

a light bulb? [*show old one*]	μία λάμπα; mee-a lamba
a plastic bucket?	ἕνα πλαστικό κουβᾶ; enna plasteeko koova
a plastic can?	ἕνα πλαστικό δοχεῖο; enna plasteeko tho-hee-o
a scouring pad?	ἕνα σύρμα γιά πιάτα; enna seerma ha pee-at-a
a spanner?	ἕνα κλειδί; enna kleeth-ee
a sponge?	ἕνα σφουγγάρι; enna sfoongar-ee
any string?	σπάγγο; spango
any tent pegs?	πάσσαλους σκηνῆς; passal-ooss skeen-eess
a tin opener?	ἕνα ἀνοικτήρι γιά κονσέρβες; enna an-eekteeree ya kon-sehr-vess
a torch?	ἕνα φάκο; enna fak-o
any torch batteries?	μπαταρίες γιά φακούς; batar-ee-ess ya fak-ooss
a universal plug (for the sink)?	ἕνα βούλωμα (γιά τό νεροχύτη); enna vooloma (ya toh nehro-heetee)
a washing line?	σκοινί γιά τό στέγνωμα τῶν ρούχων; skeenee ya toh stegnoma ton roo-hon
any washing powder?	σκόνη γιά πλύσιμο; skon-ee ya pleess-eemo
any washing up liquid?	ὑγρό γιά τά πιάτα; eegro ya ta pee-at-a
a washing-up brush?	βούρτσα γιά τά πιάτα; voortsa ya ta pee-at-a

[*For other essential expressions, see 'Shop talk', p. 58*)

Shop talk

ESSENTIAL INFORMATION

- Know your coins and bills
  coins: see illustration
  bills: 50 drachmas, 100 drachmas, 500 drachmas, 1,000 drachmas
- Know how to say the important weights and measures:

50 grams	πενῆντα γραμμάρια
	pen-*ee*nda gramm*a*-ria
100 grams	ἐκατό γραμμάρια
	ek-at-*o* gramm*a*-ria
200 grams	διακόσια γραμμάρια
	thee-ak*o*ss-ya gramm*a*-ria
½ kilo	μισό κιλό
	meesso keel*o*
1 kilo	ἕνα κιλό
	enna keel*o*
2 kilos	δύο κιλά
	thee-o keel*a*
½ litre	μισό λίτρο
	meesso leetro
1 litre	ἕνα λίτρο
	enna leetro
2 litres	δύο λίτρα
[*For numbers, see p. 125*]	thee-o leetra

[*For numbers, see p. 125*]

- There are sales in January and August when many shops give discounts of 10% on all goods.
- Bargaining is less and less common but if you feel you are being overcharged – particularly for tourist items – try suggesting a more reasonable price.
- In small shops don't be surprised, if customers, as well as the shop assistant, say 'hello' and 'goodbye' to you.

CUSTOMER

Hello	Γειά σας
	yassas
Good morning ⎤	Καλημέρα
Good day ⎥	kal-eemehra
Good afternoon (after siesta) ⎥	Καλησπέρα
Good evening ⎦	kal-eespehra
Goodbye	Γειά σας
	yassas
I'm just looking	Ρίχνω μιά ματιά
	reehno mee-a mat-ya
Excuse me	Μέ συγχωρείτε
	meh seen-horeet-eh
How much is this/that?	Πόσο κάνει αὐτό/ἐκεῖνο;
	posso kan-ee afto/ek-eeno
What is that?	Τί εἶναι ἐκεῖνο;
	tee eeneh ek-eeno
What are those?	Τί εἶναι ἐκεῖνα;
	tee eeneh ek-eena
Is there a discount?	Κάνετε ἔκπτωση;
	kan-et-eh ekptoss-ee
I'd like that, please	Θά ἤθελα ἐκεῖνο, παρακαλῶ
	tha eethalla ek-eeno parakalo
Not that	Ὄχι ἐκεῖνο
	o-hee ek-eeno
Like that	Σάν ἐκεῖνο
	san ek-eeno
That's enough, thank you	Φτάνει, εὐχαριστῶ
	ftan-ee ef-har-eesto
More, please	Περισσότερο, παρακαλῶ
	perissot-ehro parakalo
Less than that, please	Λιγότερο ἀπό αὐτό, παρακαλῶ
	leegot-ehro apo afto parakalo
That's fine ⎤	Ἐν τάξει
OK ⎦	endaksee
I won't take it, thank you	Δέν θά τό πάρω, εὐχαριστῶ
	then tha toh par-o ef-har-eesto
It's not right	Δέν εἶναι σωστό
	then eeneh sosto
Thank you very much	Εὐχαριστῶ πάρα πολύ
	ef-har-eesto para pol-ee

Have you got something . . .	Ἔχετε κάτι . . . eh-het-eh kat-ee . . .
better?	καλύτερο; kal-eet-ehro
cheaper?	φθηνότερο; ftheenot-ehro
different?	διαφορετικό; thee-afor-et-eeko
larger?	μεγαλύτερο; meg-aleet-ehro
smaller?	μικρότερο; meekrot-ehro
At what time do you . . .	Τί ὥρα . . . tee ora . . .
open?	ἀνοίγετε; aneeget-eh
close?	κλείνετε; kleenet-eh
Can I have a bag, please?	Μπορῶ νά ἔχω μία τσάντα, παρακαλῶ; boro na eh-ho mee-a tsanda parakalo
Can I have a receipt?	Μπορῶ νά ἔχω μία ἀπόδειξη; boro na eh-ho mee-a apoth-eeksee
Do you take . . .	Παίρνετε . . . pehr-net-eh . . .
English/American money?	ἐγγλέζικα/ἀμερικάνικα λεφτά; englez-eeka/amerikan-eeka lefta
travellers cheques?	τράβελερς τσέκς; travellers' cheques
credit cards?	πιστωτικές κάρτες; peestohteekess kartess
I'd like that . . .	Θά ἤθελα . . . tha eethella . . .
one like that	ἕνα σάν ἐκεῖνο enna san ek-eeno
two like that	δύο σάν ἐκεῖνο theeo san ek-eeno

SHOP ASSISTANT

Can I help you?

Μπορῶ νά σᾶς βοηθήσω;
boro na sas vo-eeth-eesso

What would you like?

Τί θά θέλατε;
tee tha thellat-eh

Will that be all?⌉
Is that all?
Anything else? ⌋

Τίποτα ἄλλο;
teepota allo

Would you like it wrapped?

Θέλετε νά σᾶς τό τυλίξω;
thellet-eh na sas toh teeleek-so

Sorry, none left

Λυπᾶμαι, δέν ἔχει μείνει
τίποτα
.leepam-eh then eh-hee meenee
teepota

I haven't got any

Δέν ἔχω
then eh-ho

I haven't got any more

Δέν μοῦ ἔχει μείνει τίποτα
then moo eh-hee meenee teepota

How many do you want?⌉
How much do you want?⌋

Πόσα θέλετε;
possa thellet-eh

Is that enough?

Φτάνει αὐτό;
ftan-ee afto

Shopping for food

Bread

ESSENTIAL INFORMATION

- Finding a baker's, see p. 22.
- Key words to look for:
  ΑΡΤΟΠΟΙΕΙΟΝ (baker's)
  ΨΩΜΙ (bread)
- Some supermarkets sell bread.
- Bakers are generally open between 7.30 a.m. to 8.30 p.m.
- All loaves are sold by weight, rolls by item.

WHAT TO SAY

Some bread, please	Ψωμί, παρακαλῶ psom-*ee* parakal*o*
A loaf (like that)	Ἕνα ψωμί (σάν ἐκείνο) enna psom-*ee* (san ek-*een*-o)
A large one	Ἕνα μεγάλο ψωμί enna megalo psom-*ee*
A small one	Ἕνα μικρό ψωμί enna meekro psom-*ee*
A bread roll	Ἕνα ψωμάκι enna psom*ak*-ee
Four bread rolls	Τέσσερα ψωμάκια tessera psom*ak*-ya
Two French-type loaves	Δύο φραντζόλες th*ee*-o frant-z*ol*-ess
½ kilo of white bread	Μισό κιλό ἄσπρο ψωμί meesso keelo aspro psom-*ee*
1 kilo of brown bread	Ἕνα κιλό ψωμί μαῦρο enna keelo psom-*ee* mavr-*o*

[*For other essential expressions, see 'Shop talk', p. 58*]

Cakes

ESSENTIAL INFORMATION

- Key words to look for:
  ΖΑΧΑΡΟΠΛΑΣΤΕΙΟΝ (a place to buy cakes and have a drink)
  ΓΑΛΑΚΤΟΠΩΛΕΙΟΝ (milk bars specializing in dairy produce,
  e.g. rice puddings, yoghurt, ice-creams etc., but which also serve
  cakes. See p. 79 for 'Ordering a drink'.)
- To find a cake shop, see p. 22.

WHAT TO SAY

The types of cake you find in the shops vary from region to region
but the following are some of the most common.

μπακλαβᾶ baklava	mille feuilles pastry with nuts and honey
καταΐφι kata-*ee*fee	fine shredded pastry with walnuts and honey
γαλακτομπούρεκο galakto-b*oo*rek-o	semolina
λουκουμάδες lookoom*ath*-ess	small doughnuts fried in oil and served with honey
σοκολατίνα sokolat*ee*na	chocolate cake
πάστα ἀμυγδάλου p*a*sta ameegth*a*l-oo	almond cake
μπουγάτσα boog*a*tsa	flaky pastry filled with custard
ριζόγαλο reez*o*galo	rice pudding
γιασούρτι ya-*oo*rtee	yoghurt

You usually buy medium sized cakes by item:

Two éclairs, please   Δύο ἐκλαίρ, παρακαλῶ
                           th*ee*-o eclair parakal*o*

You buy small cakes by weight:

200 grams of petits fours	Διακόσια γραμμάρια κουλούρια, παρακαλώ
	thee-akoss-ya gramma-ria kooloo-ria
400 grams of biscuits	Τετρακόσια γραμμάρια μπισκότα
	tetra-koss-ya gramma-ria beeskota

You may also want to say:

A selection, please	Διάφορα γλυκά, παρακαλώ
	thee-af-ora gleeka parakalo

[For other essential expressions, see 'Shop talk', p. 58]

Ice-cream and sweets

ESSENTIAL INFORMATION

- Key words to look for:
  ΠΑΓΩΤΑ (ice-cream)
  ΖΑΧΑΡΟΠΛΑΣΤΕΙΟΝ (cake shop)
  ΖΑΧΑΡΟΠΛΑΣΤΗΣ (cake/pastry maker)
- Best-known ice-cream brand names:
  ΕΒΓΑ
  ΔΕΛΤΑ
- Prepacked sweets are available in general stores, supermarkets and kiosks.
- Kiosks often have small fridges with ice-creams.

WHAT TO SAY

A . . . ice, please	Ένα παγωτό . . . παρακαλῶ
	enna pagoto . . . parakalo
vanilla	βανίλα
	vanilla
chocolate	σοκολάτα
	sokola-ta
cream	κρέμα
	krem-a
cassata	κασσάτο
	kassat-o
lemon	λεμόνι
	lemon-ee
strawberry	φράουλα
	fra-oola
cherry	βύσσινο
	veessino
Two . . . ices [*specify flavour as above*]	Δύο παγωτά . . .
	thee-o pagota . . .
A double	Ένα διπλό παγωτό
	enna theeplo pagoto
Two doubles	Δύο διπλά παγωτά
	thee-o theepla pagota

A cone	Ένα παγωτό χωνάκι
	enna pagoto honak-ee
A wafer	Ένα σάντουϊτς
	enna sandwich
A tub	Ένα κύπελλο
	enna keepello
A lollipop	Ένα γλυφιτζούρι
	enna glee-feet-zooree
A packet of ...	Ένα πακέτο ...
	enna pak-et-o ...
chewing gum	τσίχλες
	tseehles
sweets	καραμέλες
	karamel-ess
toffees	ζαχαρωτά
	za-harota
chocolates	σοκολατάκια
	sokolatak-ya
mints	μέντες
	men-tess

[For other essential expressions, see 'Shop talk', p. 58]

In the supermarket

ESSENTIAL INFORMATION

- The place to ask for: [*see p. 22*]
  ΣΟΥΠΕΡΜΑΡΚΕΤ (supermarket)
  ΠΑΝΤΟΠΩΛΕΙΟΝ (grocer's)
- Key instructions on signs in the shop:
  ΕΙΣΟΔΟΣ (entrance)
  ΕΞΟΔΟΣ (exit)
  ΑΠΑΓΟΡΕΥΕΤΑΙ Η ΕΙΣΟΔΟΣ (no entry)
  ΤΑΜΕΙΟΝ (cash desk)
  ΕΙΔΙΚΗ ΠΡΟΣΦΟΡΑ (special offer)
  ΣΕΛΦ–ΣΕΡΒΙΣ (self-service)
- Opening times vary but are generally 8.00 a.m. to 2.00 p.m. and 5.00 p.m. to 8.00 p.m.
- For non-food items, see 'Replacing equipment', p. 56.
- No need to say anything in a supermarket, but ask if you can't see what you want.

WHAT TO SAY

Excuse me, please	Μέ συγχωρεῖτε, παρακαλῶ
	meh seenhoreeteh parakalo
Where is . . .	Ποῦ εἶναι . . .
	poo eeneh . . .
the bread?	τό ψωμί;
	toh psom-*ee*
the butter?	τό βούτυρο;
	toh v*oo*teero
the cheese?	τό τυρί;
	toh teer*ee*
the chocolate?	ἡ σοκολάτα;
	ee sokol*a*-ta
the coffee?	ὁ καφές;
	o kaf-*ess*
the cooking oil?	τό λάδι γιά μαγείρεμα;
	toh l*a*th-ee ya mag-*ee*rema
the fish?	τά ψάρια;
	toh psar-*eea*

the fruit?	τά φροῦτα; ta froota
the honey?	τό μέλι; toh mel-ee
the jam?	οἱ μαρμελάδες; ee marmel-athess
the meat?	τό κρέας; toh kreh-ass
the milk?	τό γάλα; toh ga-la
the mineral water?	τό ἐμφιαλωμένο νερό; toh emfee-alomen-o nehro
the salt?	τό ἁλάτι; toh alat-ee
the sugar?	ἡ ζάχαρη; ee za-har-ee
the tea?	τό τσάϊ; toh tsa-ee
the tinned fish?	οἱ κονσέρβες μέ ψάρια; ee konsehr-vess meh psaria
the tinned fruit?	οἱ κονσέρβες μέ φροῦτα; ee konsehr-vess meh froota
the vinegar?	τό ξύδι; toh ksee-thee
the wine?	τά κρασιά; ta krass-ya
the yoghurt?	τό γιαούρτι; toh ya-oortee
Where are . . .	Ποῦ εἶναι . . . poo eeneh . . .
the biscuits?	τά μπισκότα; ta bee-skota
the crisps?	τά πατατάκια; ta patatak-ia
the eggs?	τά αὐγά; ta avga
the frozen foods?	τά καταψυγμένα τρόφιμα; ta kataps-eegmenna trof-eema
the fruit juices?	οἱ χυμοί φρούτων; ee heemee frooton
the pastas?	τά ζυμαρικά; ta zeemar-eeka

Where are ...	Πού είναι ...
	poo eeneh ...
the seafoods?	τά θαλασσινά;
	ta thalasseena
the snails?	τά σαλιγκάρια;
	ta saleengar-eea
the soft drinks?	τά ἀναψυκτικά ποτά;
	ta anaps-eek-teeka pota
the sweets?	οί καραμέλες;
	ee karamel-ess
the tinned vegetables?	οί κονσέρβες μέ λαχανικά;
	ee konsehr-vess meh la-han-eeka
the vegetables?	τά λαχανικά;
	ta la-han-eeka

[*For other essential expressions, see 'Shop talk', p. 58*]

Picnic food

ESSENTIAL INFORMATION

- Key words to look for:
  ΠΑΝΤΟΠΩΛΕΙΟΝ (grocer's)
  ΣΟΥΠΕΡΜΑΡΚΕΤ (supermarket)
  ΣΕ ΠΑΚΕΤΟ (take-away)
- Hot food to take away can be bought in restaurants and pizza houses.
- Weight guide: 4–6 oz/150 g of prepared salad per two people, if eaten as a starter to substantial meal. 3–4 oz/100 g of prepared salad per person, if to be eaten as the main part of a picnic-type meal.

WHAT TO SAY

A slice of ...	Μία φέτα ...
	mee-ä fet-a ...
Two slices of ...	Δύο φέτες ...
	thee-o fet-ess ...
ham	ζαμπόν
	zambon

garlic sausage	λουκάνικο μὲ σκόρδο
	lookan-eeko meh skortho
salami	σαλάμι
	salam-ee
mortadella	μορταδέλλα
	mortathella
100 grams of ...	Ἑκατό γραμμάρια ...
	ek-ato gramma–ria ...
150 grams of ...	Ἑκατό πενήντα γραμμάρια ...
	ek-ato pen-eenda gramma-ria ...
200 grams of ...	Διακόσια γραμμάρια ...
	thee-akoss-ya gramma-ria ...
300 grams of ...	Τριακόσια γραμμάρια ...
	tree-akoss-ya gramma-ria ...
Russian salad	ρωσική σαλάτα
	rosseekee sala-ta
olives (black/green)	ἑλιές (μαῦρες/πράσινες)
	el-ee-ess (mavr-ess/prasseen-ess)
cheese	τυρί
	teeree

You may also like to try some of these:

ταραμοσαλάτα taramo-sala-ta	cod's roe mixed with oil and lemon
φέτα fet-a	white cheese made of goat's milk
κασέρι kassehr-ee	yellow cheese, rich in cream
κεφαλοτύρι kef-aloteer-ee	very salty yellow cheese
μανούρι manooree	very creamy white cheese
μυτζήθρα meetzeethra	white soft cheese made from ewe's milk
χαλβάς halv-ass	sweet made from sesame seeds or semolina, and honey

[For other essential expressions see 'shoptalk', p. 58]

Fruit and vegetables

ESSENTIAL INFORMATION

- Key words to look for:
  ΦΡΟΥΤΑ (fruit)
  ΟΠΟΡΟΠΩΛΕΙΟΝ (greengrocer's)
  ΛΑΧΑΝΙΚΑ (vegetables)
- If possible buy fruit and vegetables in the market where they are cheaper and fresher than in the shops. Open air markets are held once or twice a week in most areas, usually in the mornings.
- It is customary for you to choose your own fruit and vegetables at the market and for the stallholder to weigh and price them. You must take your own shopping bag – paper and plastic bags are not normally provided.
- Weight guide: 1 kilo of potatoes is sufficient for six people for one meal.

WHAT TO SAY

½ kilo of . . .	Μισό κιλό . . . meesso keelo . . .
1 kilo of . . .	Ένα κιλό . . . enna keelo . . .
2 kilos of . . .	Δύο κιλά . . . thee-o keela . . .
apples	μῆλα meela
apricots	βερύκοκκα vehr-eekoka
bananas	μπανάνες banan-ess
cherries	κεράσια kehr-ass-ya
figs	σῦκα seeka
grapes (white/black)	σταφύλια (ἄσπρα/μαῦρα) staf-eel-ya (aspra/mavra)
oranges	πορτοκάλια portokal-ya

peaches	ροδάκινα
	rothak-eena
pears	αχλάδια
	a-hlath-ya
plums	δαμάσκηνα
	thamask-eena
strawberries	φράουλες
	fra-ool-ess
A pineapple, please	Έναν ανανά, παρακαλώ
	ennan anana parakalo
A grapefruit	Μία φράπα
	mee-a frap-a
A melon/water melon	Ένα πεπόνι/καρπούζι
	enna pep-on-ee/karpoozee
250 grams of . . .	Διακόσια-πενήντα γραμμάρια . . .
	thee-a-koss-ya pen-eenda gramma-ria . . .
½ kilo of . . .	Μισό κιλό . . .
	meesso keelo . . .
1 kilo of . . .	Ένα κιλό . . .
	enna keelo . . .
1½ kilos of . . .	Ενάμισο κιλό . . .
	enna-meesso keelo . . .
2 kilos of . . .	Δύο κιλά . . .
	thee-o keela . . .
aubergines	μελιτζάνες
	mel-eetzan-ess
beetroot	παντζάρια
	pannzar-eea
carrots	καροττα
	karota
courgettes	κολοκυθάκια
	kolokee-thak-ya
green beans	φασολάκια
	fassolak-ya
leeks	πράσσα
	prassa
mushrooms	μανιτάρια
	maneeta-ria
onions	κρεμμύδια
	kremmeeth-ya

2 kilos of . . .	Δύο κιλά . . .
	thee-o keela . . .
peas	μπιζέλια
	beezel-ya
peppers (green/red)	πιπεριές (πράσινες/κόκκινες)
	pee-peh-ree-ess (prasseen-ess/
	kokeen-ess)
potatoes	πατάτες
	patat-ess
spinach	σπανάκι
	spanak-ee
tomatoes	ντομάτες
	domat-ess
A bunch of . . .	Ένα ματσάκι . . .
	enna matsak-ee . . .
parsley	μαϊντανό
	may-dan-o
radishes	ραπανάκια
	rapanak-ya
A head of garlic	Ένα σκόρδο
	enna skortho
A lettuce	Ένα μαρούλι
	enna maroolee
A cauliflower	Ένα κουνουπίδι
	enna koonoopeethee
A cabbage	Ένα λάχανο
	enna la-hano
A cucumber	Ένα αγγούρι
	enna angooree
Like that, please	Όπως εκείνο, παρακαλώ
	op-oss ek-eeno parakalo

These are some fruit and vegetables with which you may not be familiar:

μούσμουλα	medlars: small slightly sour fruit,
moosmoola	orange colour, juicy, eaten raw.
κυδώνι	quince: pale yellow apple-shaped
keethon-ee	fruit, sharp, mostly served with
	sugar
μπάμιες	okra: also called 'ladies' fingers'
bam-yess	

[*For other essential expressions, see 'Shop talk', p. 58*]

Meat

ESSENTIAL INFORMATION

- Key words to look for:
  ΚΡΕΟΠΩΛΕΙΟΝ (butcher's)
  ΚΡΕΟΠΩΛΗΣ (butcher)
- Weight guide: 4–6 oz/125–200 g of meat per person for one meal.
- There are no labels on counters and supermarket displays in Greece which could help you in deciding what cut or joint to have, so you will have to ask or simply point. Do not expect, however, to find the same cuts of meat as at your butcher at home.
- Pork in Greece is of a very high quality.

WHAT TO SAY

For a joint, choose the type of meat and then say how many people it is for:

Some beef, please	Βοδινό, παρακαλῶ
	vothee-no parakalo
Some lamb	'Αρνάκι
	arnak-ee
Some pork	Χοιρινό
	heereeno
Some veal	Μοσχαρίσιο
	moss-har-ees-yo
A joint . . .	'Ένα κομμάτι . . .
	enna kommat-ee . . .
for two people	γιά δύο ἄτομα
	ya thee-o atoma
for four people	γιά τέσσερα ἄτομα
	ya tessera atoma
for six people	γιά ἔξη ἄτομα
	ya eksee atoma

For steak, liver or kidneys, do as above:

Some steak, please	Μπόν φιλέ, παρακαλῶ
	bon feeleh parakalo
Some liver	Συκωτάκια
	seekotak-ya

Some kidneys	Νεφρά nefra
Some sausages	Λουκάνικα lookan-eeka
Some mince ...	Κιμᾶ ... keema ...
for three people	γιά τρία ἄτομα ya tree-a atoma
for five people	γιά πέντε ἄτομα ya pendeh atoma

For chops do it this way:

Two veal escalopes, please	Δύο μοσχαρίσιες μπριζόλες,
	  παρακαλῶ
	Thee-o moss-ha-rees-yess
	  breezol-ess parakalo

Three pork chops	Τρεῖς χοιρινές μπριζόλες treess heereen-ess breezol-ess
Five lamb chops	Πέντε ἀρνίσιες μπριζόλες pendeh arneess-yess breezol-ess

You may also want:

A chicken	Ἕνα κοτόπουλο enna kotop-oolo
A rabbit	Ἕνα κουνέλι enna koonel-ee
A tongue	Μία γλῶσσα mee-a glossa

Other essential expressions [see also p. 58]

Please can you ...	Παρακαλῶ μπορεῖτε νά ... parakalo boreeteh na ...
mince it?	τό κάνετε κιμᾶ; toh kan-et-eh keema
dice it?	τό κόψετε; toh kopset-eh
trim the fat?	βγάλετε τό λῖπος; vgal-et-eh toh leeposs

Fish

ESSENTIAL INFORMATION

- The place to ask for: ΨAPAΔIKO (fish shop)
- Another key word to look for is: ΘΑΛΑΣΣΙΝΑ (seafood)
- Markets usually have fresh fish stalls.
- Weight guide: 8 oz/250 g minimum per person for one meal of fish bought on the bone i.e.

½ kilo/500 g	for two people
1 kilo	for four people
1½ kilos	for six people

- You will find that cod and herring are sold dried and salted: they simply require soaking in water overnight.

WHAT TO SAY

Purchase most fish by weight:

½ kilo of . . .	Μισό κιλό . . .
	meesso keelo . . .
1 kilo of . . .	Ένα κιλό . . .
	enna keelo . . .
1½ kilos of . . .	Ενάμισο κιλό . . .
	enna-meesso keelo . . .
anchovies	αντσούγες
	ants-oog-ess
grey mullet	λυθρίνια
	lee-threen-eea
mussels	μύδια
	meeth-ya
octopus	χταπόδια
	htapoth-ya
oysters	στρείδια
	streeth-ya
prawns	γαρίδες
	ga-reethess
red mullet	μπαρμπούνια
	barboon-ya
sardines	σαρδέλες
	sar-thel-ess

smelt (fried)	μαρίδες (τιγανιτές)
	ma-reethess (teeganeetess)
squid	καλαμάρια
	kalama-ria
shrimps	γαρίδες
	ga-reethess
sea bream	συναγρίδες
	seen-agreeth-ess
trout	πέστροφες
	pestrof-ess
cod	μπακαλιάρο
	bakal-ya-ro

For some shellfish and 'frying pan' fish, specify the number:

A crab, please	Ένα καβούρι, 'παρακαλῶ
	enna kavoo-ree parakalo
A lobster	Έναν ἀστακό
	ennan astako
A trout	Μία πέστροφα
	mee-a pestrofa
A sole	Μία γλῶσσα
	mee-a glossa
A mackerel	Ένα σκουμπρί
	enna skoombree
A herring	Μία ρέγγα
	mee-a renga

Other essential expressions [see also p. 58]

Please can you . . .	Παρακαλῶ μπορεῖτε νά . . .
	parakalo boreeteh na . . .
take the heads off?	βγάλετε τά κεφάλια;
	vgal-et-eh ta kef-al-ya
clean them?	τά καθαρίσετε;
	ta katha-reeset-eh
fillet them?	βγάλετε τά κοκκάλα;
	vgal-et-eh ta kok-al-a

Eating and drinking out

Ordering a drink

ESSENTIAL INFORMATION
- The places to ask for: ΜΠΑΡ (bar), ΣΝΑΚ–ΜΠΑΡ (snack bar),
  ΟΥΖΕΡΙ (bar which serves hors d'oeuvres)
  ΖΑΧΑΡΟΠΛΑΣΤΕΙΟ (pastry shop which serves drinks as well)
  ΚΑΦΕΝΕΙΟ (coffee house, where Greek women are rarely seen)
- By law the price list (ΤΙΜΟΛΟΓΙΟΝ) must be on display.
  Service is usually included.
- Bars open late in the afternoon and close at 2.00 a.m.
  All other establishments are normally open all day.
- Bars and cafés serve both non-alcoholic and alcoholic drinks.
  Children are allowed in.
- Greek beer comes in small bottles of 350 g (about ½ pint) and
  500 g (about 1 pint).
- Greek coffee is made by heating water, mixing in the ground
  coffee and sugar, and bringing it to the boil – it is very strong.

WHAT TO SAY

I'll have . . . please	Θέλω . . . παρακαλῶ
	thello . . . parakalo
a black coffee	ἕνα νέσκαφε σκέτο
	enna nescafe sket-o
. a coffee with milk	ἕνα καφέ μέ γάλα
	enna kaf-eh meh ga-la
a Greek coffee	ἕνα Ἑλληνικό καφέ
	enna elleen-eeko kaf-eh
without sugar	σκέτο
	sket-o
medium sweet	μέτριο
	metrio
sweet	γλυκό
	gleeko
a tea	ἕνα τσάϊ
	enna tsa-ee
with milk	μέ γάλα
	meh ga-la
with lemon	μέ λεμόνι
	meh lem-on-ee

I'll have . . . please	Θέλω . . . παρακαλῶ thello . . . parakalo
a glass of milk	ἕνα ποτήρι γάλα enna poteeree ga-la
a hot chocolate	μία ζεστή σοκολάτα mee-a zestee sokola-ta
an iced coffee	ἕνα νέσκαφε φραπέ enna nescafe frap-eh
a mineral water	ἐμφιαλωμένο νερό emfee-alomen-o nehro
a lemonade	μία λεμονάδα mee-a lem-on-atha
a lemon squash	μία λεμονάδα χυμό mee-a lem-on-atha heemo
a Coca-Cola	μία κόκα κόλα mee-a koka kola
an orangeade	μία πορτοκαλάδα mee-a portokal-atha
an orange juice	μία πορτοκαλάδα χυμό mee-a portokal-atha heemo
a pineapple juice	ἕναν ἀνανᾶ χυμό ennan anana heemo
a beer	μία μπύρα mee-a bee-ra
a large bottle	ἕνα μεγάλο μπουκάλι enna megalo bookalee
a small bottle	ἕνα μικρό μπουκάλι enna meekro bookal-ee
A glass of . . .	Ἕνα ποτήρι . . . enna poteeree . . .
Two glasses of . . .	Δύο ποτήρια . . . thee-o poteeria . . .
A bottle of . . .	Ἕνα μπουκάλι . . . enna bookal-ee . . .
Two bottles of . . .	Δύο μπουκάλια . . . thee-o bookal-ya . . .
red wine	κόκκινο κρασί kokino krassee
white wine	ἄσπρο κρασί aspro krassee
rosé wine	ροζέ roz-eh

dry	ξυρό
	kseero
sweet	γλυκό
	gleeko
champagne	σαμπάνια
	sampan-ya
A whisky	Ἕνα οὐίσκι
	enna oo-eeskee
with ice	μέ πάγο
	meh pag-o
with water	μέ νερό
	meh nehro
with soda	μέ σόδα
	meh sotha
A gin	Ἕνα τζίν
	enna gin
with tonic	μέ τόνικ
	meh ton-ic
with lemon	μέ λεμόνι
	meh lem-on-ee
A brandy	Ἕνα κονιάκ
	enna konyak

These are local drinks you may like to try:

ρετσίνα	a resinated wine (the resin added
ret-seena	to the vats during fermentation gives this white wine its distinctive flavour)
μαυροδάφνη	a dessert wine (sweet and dark)
mavro-thafnee	
οὖζο	an aniseed-flavoured aperitif
oozo	
μαστίχα	a sweet aperitif flavoured with
masteeeha	mastic (the resin from the lentisk tree)
κουμκουάτ	a liqueur made from tiny oranges:
koom-koo-at	a speciality of Corfu
βυσσινάδα	a soft drink made from cherries
vees-seen-atha	

Other essential expressions:

Miss! [*This does not sound abrupt in Greek*]	Δεσποινίς!
	thespeen-*eess*
Waiter!	Γκαρσόν!
	garson
The bill, please	Τό λογαριασμό, παρακαλώ
	toh logaree-azmo parakalo
How much does that come to?	Πόσο κάνει;
	posso kan-ee
Is service included?	Εἶναι μέ τό σερβίς;
	eeneh meh toh serveess
Where is the toilet, please?	Ποῦ εἶναι ἡ τουαλέτα, παρακαλώ;
	poo eeneh ee too-al-et-a parakalo

Ordering a snack

ESSENTIAL INFORMATION

- Look for a café or small shop with any of the following signs:
  ΣΝΑΚ-ΜΠΑΡ (snack bar)
  ΟΥΖΕΡΙ (bar which serves hors d'oeuvres)
  ΚΑΦΕΝΕΙΟ (coffee house)
- Look for the names of snacks (listed below) on signs in the window
  or inside on the walls e.g.
  ΤΥΡΟΠΙΤΕΣ (cheese pies)
- For cakes, see p. 64.
- For ice-cream, see p. 66.
- For picnic-type snacks, see p. 70.
- For ordering a drink, see p. 79.

WHAT TO SAY

I'll have . . . please	Θέλω . . . παρακαλῶ
	thello . . . parakalo
a cheese sandwich	ἕνα σάντουϊτς μέ τυρί
	enna sandwich meh teeree
a ham sandwich	ἕνα σάντουϊτς μέ ζαμπόν
	enna sandwich meh zambon
a meat pie	μία κρεατόπιττα
	mee-a kreh-at-op-ita
a spinach pie	μία σπανακόπιττα
	meea-a spanak-op-ita
a cheese pie	μία τυρόπιττα
	mee-a teer-op-ita
a hot dog	ἕνα χότ ντόγκ
	enna hot dog

This is another snack you may like to try:

ἕνα σουβλάκι	pieces of grilled meat wrapped in a
enna soovlak-ee	type of pancake; doner kebab

In a restaurant

ESSENTIAL INFORMATION

- To find a restaurant, see p. 22.
- You can eat at the following places:
  ΕΣΤΙΑΤΟΡΙΟΝ (restaurant)
  ΤΑΒΕΡΝΑ (typical Greek restaurant)
  ΨΑΡΟΤΑΒΕΡΝΑ (restaurant specialising in seafood)
  ΨΗΣΤΑΡΙΑ (restaurant specialising in charcoal-grilled food)
- In smaller restaurants there may be no printed menu, so you will either have to ask what is available or look at the food displayed and point. The Greeks themselves often go into the kitchen to choose their meal.
- If the menu lists two prices for each item, the second price includes a 10% service charge, but an extra tip is always welcome.
- If there is a wine waiter (he will also serve the water and bread), a small tip should be left for him on the table (not on the plate with the bill).
- Times when restaurants stay open depend on the area and the season. However, they are normally open from midday to 4.00 p.m. and 8.00 p.m. to midnight. Although Greeks tend to eat late in the summer, all restaurants, bars and cafés are obliged by law to close at 2.00 a.m.
- In most tavernas and many restaurants draught wine is available. It is served in small cans and sold by weight. Order 1 kilo (1 litre), ½ kilo (½ litre) or ¼ kilo (a large glass).

WHAT TO SAY

May I book a table?	Μπορῶ νά κλείσω ἕνα τραπέζι;
	boro na kleeso enna trap-ez-ee
I've booked a table	Ἔχω κλείσει τραπέζι
	eh-ho kleessee trap-ez-ee
A table ...	Ἕνα τραπέζι ...
	enna trap-ez-ee ...
for one	γιά ἕναν
	ya ennan
for three	γιά τρεῖς
	ya treess

The menu, please	Τόν κατάλογο παρακαλῶ
	ton katalogo parakalo
What's this please? [*point to the menu*]	Τί εἶναι αὐτό παρακαλῶ;
	tee eeneh afto parakalo
1 kilo of wine	Ἕνα κιλό κρασί
	enna keelo krassee
½ kilo of wine	Μισό κιλό κρασί
	meeso keelo krassee
¼ kilo of wine	Τέταρτο κρασί
	tetartoh krassee
A glass	Ἕνα ποτήρι
	enna poteeree
A bottle	Ἕνα μπουκάλι
	enna bookal-ee
A half bottle	Ἕνα μικρό μπουκάλι
	enna meekro bookal-ee
Red/white/rosé	Κόκκινο/ἄσπρο/ροζέ
	kokino/aspro/roz-eh
Some more bread, please	'Ακόμα ψωμί, παρακαλῶ
	akoma psom-ee parakalo
Some more wine	ἀκόμα κρασί
	akoma krassee
Some oil	Λίγο λάδι
	leego la-thee
Some vinegar	Λίγο ξύδι
	leego ksee-thee
Some salt/pepper	Λίγο ἁλάτι/πιπέρι
	leego alat-ee/peepeh-ree
With/without garlic	μέ/χωρίς σκόρδο
	meh/hor-eess skortho
Some water	Λίγο νερό
	leego nehro
How much does that come to?	Πόσο κάνει;
	posso kan-ee
Is service included	Εἶναι μέ τό σερβίς;
	eeneh meh toh serveess
Where is the toilet, please?	Ποῦ εἶναι ἡ τουαλέτα, παρακαλῶ;
	poo eeneh ee too-al-et-a parakalo
Miss! [*This does not sound abrupt in Greek*]	Δεσποινίς!
	thespeen-eess
Waiter!	Γκαρσόν!
	garson
The bill, please	Τό λογαριασμό, παρακαλῶ
	toh logaree-azmo parakalo

Key words for courses, as seen on some menus
[*Only ask this if you want the waiter to remind you of the choice.*]

What have you got in the way of . . .	Τί . . . ἔχετε; tee . . . eh-het-eh
STARTERS?	ΟΡΕΚΤΙΚΑ orekteeka
SOUP?	ΣΟΥΠΕΣ soopess
EGG?	ΑΥΓΑ avgah
FISH?	ΨΑΡΙΑ psareea
MEAT?	ΚΡΕΑΣ kreass
GAME?	ΚΥΝΗΓΙ keeneegee
FOWL?	ΠΟΥΛΕΡΙΚΑ poolereeka
VEGETABLES?	ΛΑΧΑΝΙΚΑ lahaneeka
CHEESE?	ΤΥΡΙΑ teereea
FRUIT?	ΦΡΟΥΤΑ froota
ICE-CREAM?	ΠΑΓΩΤΑ pagota
DESSERT?	ΓΛΥΚΑ gleeka

UNDERSTANDING THE MENU

You will find the names of the principal ingredients of most dishes
on these pages:

Starters	p. 70	Fruit	p. 72
Meat	p. 75	Cheese	p. 70
Fish	p. 77	Ice-cream	p. 66
Vegetables	p. 72	Dessert	p. 64

Used together with the following lists of cooking and menu terms
they should help you to decode the menu.

Cooking and menu terms

Βραστό vrasto	boiled, poached, stewed
γεμιστό ghemeesto	stuffed
ζεστό zesto	hot
καπνιστό kapneesto	smoked
στά κάρβουνα sta karvoona	charcoal-grilled
τῆς κατσαρόλας teess katsar-olass	en casserole
κοκκινιστό kokkin-eesto	cooked with oil and tomatoes
σενιάν (κρέας) sen-yan (kreh-ass)	rare (meat)
μέτρια ψημένο metria pseemen-o	medium
καλοψημένο kalops-eemen-o	well-done
κρύο kree-o	cold
μέ μαϊντανό meh may-dan-o	with parsley
μαρινάτο mareenato	marinated
παστό pasto	cured
πουρέ poo-reh	mashed (potatoes)
μέ σάλτσα meh saltsa	with sauce
στή σχάρα stee skar-a	grilled
τηγανισμένο σέ πολύ λάδι teegan-eesmen-o seh pol-ee la-thee	deep fried

τηγανητό teegan-eeto	fried
τριμμένο trimmen-o	grated
στό φοῦρνο sto foorno	baked
ψητό pseeto	roasted, baked
ψητό τῆς κατσαρόλας pseeto teess katsar-olass	pot-roasted
ψηλοκομμένο psee-lokommen-o	finely chopped
ὠμό om-o	raw

Further words to help you understand the menu

ἀγγοῦρι angooree	cucumber
αὐγολέμονο avgol-em-ono	rice, egg and lemon soup
γαριδοσαλάτα gareeth-osala-ta	shrimps in oil and lemon sauce
γιουβαρλάκια yoo-varlak-ya	minced meat and rice balls
γιουβέτσι yoo-vet-see	meat with noodles baked in the oven
κεφτέδες kefteth-ess	meatballs made with bread and herbs
κοκορέτσι kokoret-see	lamb innards roasted on a spit
κρεμμύδι kremmeethee	onion
μελιτζάνες γεμιστές mel-eetzan-ess ghe-meess-tess	stuffed aubergines
μουσακά moossaka	layers of baked aubergines and minced meat
μπιζέλια beezel-ya	peas
μπιφτέκια beeftekya	grilled meatballs
ντολμάδες dolmath-ess	vine or cabbage leaves stuffed with rice and/or meat

ντομάτες γεμιστές domat-ess ghemeess-tess	stuffed tomatoes with rice and/or minced meat
παστίτσιο pasteetsio	minced meat and macaroni baked and completed by a sauce
παστουρμάς pastoorm-ass	heavily spiced, dried or smoked meat
πατσάς patsass	tripe soup
πιπεριές γεμιστές peepeh-ree-ess ghemeess-tess	stuffed peppers
ρεβύθια reh-veethia	chick-peas
σκορδαλιά skor-thal-ya	garlic sauce
σκόρδο skortho	garlic
σουβλάκι soovlak-ee	cubes of meat grilled on a spit
σουτζουκάκια soot-zookak-ya	spicy meatballs in sauce
ταραμοσαλάτα taramo-sala-ta	salad of fish roe blended with bread, oil and lemon
τζατζίκι tsat-zeekee	salad of yoghurt, cucumber, garlic, olive oil and mint
φακιές fak-yess	lentils
φασολάδα fassol-atha	kidney bean soup with tomatoes
χόρτα σαλάτα horta sala-ta	made from greens resembling spinach
χυλόπιττες heelop-eet-ess	noodles
χωριάτικη σαλάτα horeeat-eekee sala-ta	mixed salad, (tomatoes, cucumber, green peppers, cheese, onion)
ψαρόσουπα psaross-oopa	fish soup

Health

ESSENTIAL INFORMATION

- At present there are no reciprocal health agreements between the US and Greece. Moreover, the public health sector offers an extremely limited service. It is *essential* to have proper medical insurance. A policy can be bought through a travel agent, a broker or a motoring organization.
- Take your own 'first line' first aid kit with you.
- See p. 44 for minor disorders and treatment at a chemist's.
- See p. 22 for asking the way to a doctor, dentist, or chemist.
- Once in Greece decide on a definite plan of action in case of serious illness: communicate your problem to a near neighbour, the receptionist or someone you see regularly. You are then dependent on that person helping you obtain treatment.
- To find a doctor in an emergency, look for: ΝΟΣΟΚΟΜΕΙΟΝ (hospital) or contact the police.
- Because of the limited ambulance service in Greece, taxis are frequently used to take people to the hospital.

What's the matter?

I have a pain in my ...	Μοῦ πονάει ... moo pona-ee. ..
abdomen	τό στομάχι toh stomahee
ankle	ὁ ἀστράγαλος o astragal-oss
arm	τό χέρι toh hehree
back	ἡ πλάτη ee plat-ee
bladder	ἡ κύστις ee keesteess
bowels	τό ἔντερο toh endero
breast/chest	τό στῆθος toh steethoss
ear	τό αὐτί toh aftee

eye	τό μάτι
	toh mat-ee
foot	τό πόδι
	toh poth-ee
head	τό κεφάλι
	toh kef-al-ee
heel	ή φτέρνα
	ee ftehr-na
jaw	τό σαγῶνι
	toh sag-on-ee
kidney	τό νεφρό
	toh nefro
leg	τό πόδι
	toh po-thee
lung	ό πνεύμων
	o pnevmon
neck	ό λαιμός
	o lem-oss
penis	τό πέος
	toh peh-oss
shoulder	ή ώμοπλάτη
	ee omo-plat-ee
stomach	τό στομάχι
	toh stoma-hee
testicle	ό ὄρχις
	o orheess
throat	ό λαιμός
	o lem-oss
vagina	ό κόλπος
	o kolposs
wrist	ό καρπός τοῦ χεριοῦ
	o karposs too hehr-ee-oo
I have a pain here [point]	Ἔχω ἕνα πόνο ἐδῶ
	eh-ho enna pon-o eth-o
I have toothache	Ἔχω πονόδοντο
	eh-ho pon-othondo
I have broken . . .	Ἔσπασα . . .
	espassa . . .
my dentures	τή μασέλα μου
	tee massella moo
my glasses	τά γυαλιά μου
	ta yal-ya moo

I have lost . . .	Ἔχασα . . .
	eh-hassa . . .
my contact lenses	τούς φακούς ἐπαφῆς μου
	tooss fak-ooss ep-afeess moo
a filling	ἕνα σφράγισμα
	enna sfrag-eesma
My child is ill	Τό παιδί μου εἶναι ἄρρωστο
	toh peth-ee moo eeneh arrosto
He/she has a pain in his/her. . .	Τοῦ/Τῆς πονάει . . .
	too/teess pona-ee . . .
ankle [see list above]	ὁ ἀστράγαλος
	o astragal-oss
How bad is it?	
I'm ill	Εἶμαι ἄρρωστος/ἄρρωστη*
	eemeh arrostoss/arrostee*
It's urgent	Εἶναι ἐπεῖγον
	eeneh ep-eegon
It's serious	Εἶναι σοβαρό
	eeneh sovaro
It's not serious	Δέν εἶναι σοβαρό
	then eeneh sovaro
It hurts	Πονάει
	pona-ee
It hurts a lot	Πονάει πολύ
	pona-ee pol-ee
It doesn't hurt much	Δέν πονάει πολύ
	then pona-ee pol-ee
The pain occurs . . .	Ὁ πόνος ἔρχεται . . .
	o pon-oss ehr-het-eh . . .
every quarter of an hour	κάθε τέταρτο
	kath-eh tet-arto
every half hour	κάθε μισύ ὥρα
	kath-eh meessee ora
every hour	κάθε ὥρα
	kath-eh ora
every day	κάθε μέρα
	kath-eh mehra
most of the time	τίς περισσότερες φορές
	teess perissot-ehress for-ess
I've had it for . . .	Τόν ἔχω ἐδῶ καί . . .
	ton eh-ho eth-o keh . . .

*For men use the first alternative, for women the second

one hour/one day	μία ὥρα/μία μέρα
	mee-a ora/mee-a mehra
two hours/two days	δύο ὥρες/δύο μέρες
	thee-o or-ess/thee-o mehr-ess
It's a . . .	Εἶναι ἕνας . . .
	eeneh ennass . . .
sharp pain	ξαφνικός πόνος
	ksaf-neek-oss pon-oss
dull pain	μέτριος πόνος
	met-ree-os pon-oss
nagging pain	ἐνοχλητικός πόνος
	enno-hleet-eekoss pon-oss
I feel . . .	Αἰσθάνομαι . . .
	es-than-om-eh . . .
dizzy	μία ζάλη
	mee-a zal-ee
sick	μία τάση γιά ἐμετό
	mee-a tassee ya em-et-o
weak	μία ἀδυναμία
	mee-a a-theen-amee-ya
feverish	νά ἔχω πυρετό
	na eh-ho peeret-o

Already under treatment for something else?

I take . . . regularly [*show*]	Παίρνω συνήθως . . .
	pehr-no seeneeth-oss . . .
this medicine	αὐτό τό φάρμακο
	afto toh farmako
these pills	αὐτά τά χάπια
	afta ta hap-ya
I have . . .	Ἔχω . . .
	eh-ho . . .
haemorrhoids	αἱμορροΐδες
	em-orro-eethess
rheumatism	ρευματισμούς
	revma-teezmooss
I'm . . .	Εἶμαι . . .
	eemeh . . .
diabetic	διαβητικός/διαβητική*
	thee-av-eeteek-oss/thee-av-eeteek-ee*

*For men use the first alternative, for women the second

I'm . . .	Εἶμαι . . .
	*ee*meh . . .
asthmatic	ἀσθματικός/ἀσθματική*
	as-thmat-eek-*oss*/as-thmat-eek-*ee**
pregnant	ἔγκυος
	engee-oss
I have a heart condition	Εἶμαι καρδιακός/καρδιακή*
	*ee*meh karthee-akoss/karthee-akee*
I am allergic to (pencillin)	Εἶμαι ἀλλεργικός/ἀλλεργική* στή (πενικιλλίνη)
	*ee*meh allehr-geek-*oss*/ allehr-geek-*ee* stee (pen-eekeel-*ee*nee)

Other essential expressions

Please can you help?	Μπορεῖτε νά με βοηθήσετε σᾶς παρακαλῶ;
	bor*ee*teh na meh vo-eeth-*ee*sset-eh sas parakalo
A doctor, please	Ἕνα γιατρό, παρακαλῶ
	enna yatro parakalo
A dentist	Ἕνα ὀδοντογιατρό
	enna othondo-yatro
I don't speak Greek	Δέν μιλῶ Ἑλληνικά
	then meelo elleen-eek*a*
What time does . . . arrive?	Τί ὥρα ἔρχεται . . .
	tee ora erheteh . . .
the doctor	ὁ γιατρός;
	o yatross
the dentist	ὁ ὀδοντογιατρός;
	o othondo-yatross

From the doctor: key sentences to understand

Take this . . .	Νά παίρνετε αὐτό . . .
	na pehr-net-eh afto . . .
every day/hour	κάθε μέρα/ὥρα
	kath-eh mehra/ora
twice/four times a day	δύο/τέσσερες φορές τή μέρα
	thee-o/tesser-ess for-ess tee mer-a
Stay in bed	Μείνετε στό κρεββάτι
	meenet-eh sto krevvat-ee

*For men use the first alternative, for women the second

Don't travel	Μή ταξιδεύετε
	mee taksee-theh-vet-eh
for . . . days/weeks	γιά . . . μέρες/βδομάδες
	ya . . . mehr-ess/vthom-ath-ess
You must go to hospital	Πρέπει νά πᾶτε στό νοσοκομείο
	prep-ee na pat-eh sto
	nossokomee-o

Problems: complaints, loss, theft

ESSENTIAL INFORMATION

- Problems with:
  camping facilities, see p. 38.
  household appliances, see p. 41.
  health, see p. 90
  the car, see p. 104.
- If the worst comes to the worst, find the police station, to ask the way, see p. 22.
- Look for:
  ΑΣΤΥΝΟΜΙΑ (police in towns) or this sign

- or ΧΩΡΟΦΥΛΑΚΗ (gendarmerie, i.e. rural police)
- If you lose your passport go to your nearest Consulate.
- In an emergency, dial 100 for the police.

COMPLAINTS

I bought this . . .	Ἀγόρασα αὐτό . . .
	agorassa aft*o* . . .
today	σήμερα
	seemera
yesterday	χθές
	hthess
on Monday [see p. 129]	τή Δευτέρα
	tee theftehra
It's no good	Δέν εἶναι καλό
	then *eeneh* kal*o*
Look	Κυττᾶξτε
	keetaks-teh
Here [point]	Ἐδῶ
	eth-*o*
Can you . . .	Μπορεῖτε νά τό . . .
	boreeteh na toh . . .
change it?	ἀλλάξετε;
	all*a*k-set-eh
mend it?	ἐπισκευάσετε;
	ep-eeskev-*a*sset-eh
Here's the receipt	Ὁρίστε ἡ ἀπόδειξη
	oreesteh ee apotheek-see
Can I have a refund?	Μπορεῖτε νά μοῦ ἐπιστρέψετε τά χρήματα;
	boreeteh na moo ep-eestrepset-eh ta hreemata
Can I see the manager?	Μπορῶ νά δῶ τόν διευθυντή;
	boro na tho ton thee-ef-theen-*tee*

LOSS
[See also 'Theft' below; the lists are interchangeable]

I have lost . . .	Ἔχασα . . .
	eh-hassa . . .
my bag	τήν τσάντα μου
	teen tsanda moo
my bracelet	τό βραχιόλι μου
	toh vra-hee-*o*lee moo
my camera	τήν φωτογραφική μηχανή μου
	teen fotograffeekee meehanee moo
my car logbook	τήν ἄδεια κυκλοφορίας
	teen ath-eya keek-loforee-ass

my driving licence	τήν ἄδεια ὁδηγήσεως
	teen athee-a othee-geess-eh-oss
my insurance certificate	τήν ἀσφάλεια τοῦ αὐτοκινήτου μου
	teen asfal-ya too aftokeen-eetoo moo
my jewellery	τά κοσμήματα μου
	ta kosmeem-ata moo
everything	τά πάντα
	ta panda

THEFT
[See also 'Loss' above; the lists are interchangeable]

Someone has stolen . . .	Κάποιος μοῦ ἔκλεψε . . .
	kap-ee-oss moo eklepseh . . .
my car	τό αὐτοκίνητο μου
	toh aftokeen-eeto moo
my car radio	Τό ράδιό τοῦ αὐτοκινήτου μου
	toh rath-yo too aftkokeen-eetoo moo
my car keys	τά κλειδιά τοῦ αὐτοκινήτου μου
	ta kleeth-ya too aftokeen-eetoo moo
my keys	τά κλειδιά μου
	ta kleeth-ya moo
my money	τά χρήματα μου
	ta hreem-ata moo
my necklace	τό κολλιέ μου
	toh kollee-eh moo
my passport	τό διαβατήριο μου
	toh thee-avateeree-o moo
my radio	τό ράδιο μου
	toh rath-yo moo
my tickets	τά εἰσιτήρια μου
	ta eess-eeteeree-a moo
my travellers' cheques	τά τράβελερς τσέκς μου
	ta travellers' cheques moo
my wallet	τό πορτοφόλι μου
	toh portofol-ee moo
my watch	τό ρολόϊ μου
	toh rolo-ee moo
my luggage	τά πράγματα μου
	ta pragmata moo

LIKELY REACTIONS: key words to understand

Wait	Περιμένετε perimen-et-eh
When?	Πότε; pot-eh
Where?	Πoῦ; poo
Name?	Ὄνομα; onoma
Address?	Διεύθυνση; thee-ef-theen-see
I can't help you	Δέν μπορῶ νά σᾶς βοηθήσω then boro na sas vo-ee-theessa
Nothing to do with me	Δέν μπορῶ νά κάνω τίποτα then boro na kano teepota

The post office

ESSENTIAL INFORMATION

- To find a post office, see p. 22.
- Key words to look for:
  ΤΑΧΥΔΡΟΜΕΙΟΝ (post office)
  ΕΛ.ΤΑ. (abbreviation for Greek
  post office: look out for this symbol)
  ΟΤΕ (telecommunications)
- For stamps, look for the word
  ΓΡΑΜΜΑΤΟΣΗΜΑ.
- Stamps are also sold in kiosks.
- Letter boxes are yellow.
- For post restante you should show
  your passport at the counter marked
  ΠΟΣΤ ΡΕΣΤΑΝΤ in the main post office.
- Telegrams are not sent from post offices, but from the offices of
  the OTE, the telecommunications company of Greece.

WHAT TO SAY

To England, please	Γιά τήν 'Αγγλία, παρακαλῶ
	ya teen anglee-a parakalo

[Hand letters, cards or parcels over the counter]

To Australia	Γιά τήν Αὐστραλία
	ya teen af-straleea
To the United States	Γιά τήν 'Αμερική
	ya teen amerik-ee

[For other countries, see p. 134]

How much is . . .	Πόσο κάνει . . .
	posso kan-ee . . .
this parcel (to Canada)?	αὐτό τό δέμα (γιά τόν Καναδᾶ);
	afto toh them-a (ya ton kana-tha)
a letter (to Australia)?	ἕνα γράμμα (γιά τήν Αὐστραλία);
	enna gramma (ya teen af-stralee-a)
a postcard (to England)?	μία κάρτα (γιά τήν 'Αγγλία);
	mee-a karta (ya teen anglee-a)
Airmail	'Αεροπορικῶς
	ehroporeek-oss
Surface mail	'Απλό
	aplo
One stamp, please	Ἕνα γραμματόσημο, παρακαλῶ
	enna grammat-oss-eemo parakalo
Two stamps	Δύο γραμματόσημα
	thee-o grammat-oss-eema
One (10) drachma stamp	Ἕνα γραμματόσημο (τῶν δέκα) δραχμῶν
	enna grammat-oss-eemo (ton theh-ka) thra-hmon

Telephoning

ESSENTIAL INFORMATION

- Unless you read and speak Greek well, it's best not to make phone calls by yourself. Go to OTE (Telecommunications Organization of Greece, look out for this symbol) – and not to the post office – and write the town and number you want on a piece of paper.
- Add ΠΡΟΣΩΠΙΚΟ ΤΗΛΕΦΩΝΗΜΑ if you want a person-to-person call, or ΝΑ ΧΡΕΩΘΕΙ ΤΟ ΤΗΛΕΦΩΝΗΜΑ ΣΤΟΝ ΠΑΡ-ΑΛΗΠΤΗ if you want to reverse the charges.
- The number of public phones is rather limited in Greece. However, almost all kiosks and a number of cafés have phones for the public. Phones in cafés have meters and you pay after phoning according to the number of units used. The few public phone boxes are blue for local calls and orange for long distance and use normal currency not tokens.
- To ask the way to a telephone, see p. 22.
- Look for these signs:
  ΤΗΛΕΦΩΝΟ ΔΙΑ ΤΟ ΚΟΙΝΟ (public telephone)
  ΕΔΩ ΤΗΛΕΦΩΝΕΙΤΕ (telephone here)
- OTE phones must be used for all international calls.
- To phone the UK from Greece, dial 0044 and then the number you want.
- To phone the USA, the code is 001.

WHAT TO SAY

Where can I make a telephone call?	Πού μπορῶ νά κάνω ἕνα τηλέφωνο;
	poo boro na kan-o enna teelefono
Local/abroad	Τοπικό/γιά τό ἐξωτερικό
	top-eeko/ya toh eksot-ehreeko

I'd like this number . . .	Θέλω αὐτό τόν ἀριθμό . . .
[*show number*]	thello afto ton a-reethmo . . .
in England	στήν Ἀγγλία
	steen angleea
in Canada	στόν Καναδᾶ
	ston kana-tha
in the USA	στήν Ἀμερική
	steen amerik-ee
[*For other countries, see p. 134*]	
Can you dial it for me, please?	Μπορεῖτε νά μοῦ πάρετε τόν ἀριθμό, σᾶς παρακαλῶ;
	boreeteh na moo par-et-eh ton a-reethmo sas parakalo
How much is it?	Πόσο κάνει;
	posso kan-ee
Hello	Ναί
	neh
May I speak to . . .?	Μοῦ δίνετε . . .;
	moo theenet-eh . . .
Extension . . .	Ἐσωτερικό . . .
	es-otehreeko . . .
I'm sorry, I don't speak Greek	Λυπᾶμαι, δέν μιλάω Ἑλληνικά
	leepam-eh then meela-o elleen-eeka
Do you speak English?	Μιλᾶτε Ἀγγλικά;
	meelat-eh angleeka
Goodbye	Χαίρετε
	hch-ret-eh
I'd like to send a telegram	Θέλω νά στείλω ἕνα τηλεγράφημα
	thello na steelo enna teelegraf-eema

LIKELY REACTIONS

That's (45) drachmas	(Σαράντα πέντε) δραχμές
	(saranda pendeh) thra-hmess
Cabin number (3)	Θάλαμος νουμερο (τρία)
[*For numbers, see p. 125*]	thalamoss noomero (treea)
Don't hang up	Μήν κλείσετε
	meen kleesset-eh

I'm trying to connect you	Προσπαθῶ νά σᾶς συνδέσω
	prospatho na sas seen-theh-so
You're through	Μιλᾶτε
	meelat-eh
There's a delay	Ὑπάρχει καθυστέρηση
	eepar-hee kathee-stehr-eessee
I'll try again	Θά προσπαθήσω ξανά
	tha prospatheesso ksana

Changing cheques and money

ESSENTIAL INFORMATION

- Finding your way to a bank of change bureau, see p. 22.
- Look for these signs:
  ΤΡΑΠΕΖΑ (bank)
  BUREAU DE CHANGE (change bureau)
- To cash your normal cheques, exactly as at home, use your banker's card where you see the Eurocheque sign. Write in English, in pounds.
- Exchange rate information shows the pound as: £ . It is also quite often simply shown by the British flag.
- Have your passport handy.
- Banks are open between 8.00 a.m. and 2.00 p.m. except on Saturdays, Sundays and public holidays. However, during the high season some banks will remain open during the afternoons.

WHAT TO SAY

I'd like to cash . . .	Θέλω νά ἐξαργυρώσω . . .
	thello na ek-sarg-eerosso . . .
this travellers' cheque	αὐτό τό τράβελερς τσέκ
	afto toh travellers' cheque
these travellers' cheques	αὐτά τά τράβελερς τσέκ
	afta ta travellers' cheques
this cheque	αὐτό τό τσέκ
	afto toh cheque

I'd like to change this into drachmas	Θά ἤθελα νά ἀλλάξω αὐτό σέ δραχμές tha *ee*thella na all*a*kso *a*fto seh thra-hm*ess*
Here's ...	Ὁρίστε ... or*ee*steh ...
my banker's card	ἡ τραπεζική μου κάρτα ee trap-ez-eek*ee* moo k*a*rta
my passport	τό διαβατήριο μου toh thee-avat*ee*ree-o moo

For excursions into neighbouring countries

I'd like to change this ... [show banknotes]	Θέλω νά ἀλλάξω αὐτό ... th*e*llo na all*a*kso *a*fto ...
into Italian lira	σέ Ἰταλικές λιρέττες seh eetal-eek*ess* leeret-*ess*
into Turkish pounds	σέ τούρκικες λίρες seh t*oo*r-keekess leer*ess*
into Yugoslav dinar	σέ γιουγκοσλαυικά δηνάρια seh yoogoslavika deen*a*reeya
What is the rate of exchange?	Ποία εἶναι ἡ τιμή συναλλάγματος; p*ee*a *ee*neh ee teem*ee* seen-allagmat-*oss*

LIKELY REACTIONS

Passport, please	Τό διαβατήριο σας, παρακαλῶ toh thee-avat*ee*ree-o sas parakal*o*
Sign here	Ὑπογράψετε ἐδῶ eepogr*a*p-set-eh eth-*o*
Your banker's card, please	Τήν τραπεζική σας κάρτα, παρακαλῶ teen trap-ez-eek*ee* sas k*a*rta parakal*o*
Go to the cash desk	Πηγαίνετε στό ταμεῖο peeg-*e*n-et-eh sto tam-*ee*-o

Car travel

ESSENTIAL INFORMATION

- Finding a filling station or garage, see p. 22.
- Is it a self-service filling station? Look out for:
  ΣΕΛΦ-ΣΕΡΒΙΣ
- Grades of gasoline: ΣΟΥΠΕΡ (premium)
  BENZINH (gas) ΔΙΧΡΟΝΟ (two stroke)
  ΑΠΛΗ (standard) ΝΤΗΖΕΛ (diesel)
- One gallon is about 4½ litres (accurate enough up to 6 gallons).
- Most filling stations in Greece (ΓΚΑΡΑΖ) do not do major repairs.
  The place to go for repairs is ΣΥΝΕΡΓΕΙΟΝ
- The Greek Automobile and Touring Club (ELPA) offers assistance
  to foreign motorists free of charge.
- Dial 104 for assistance in Athens and Thessaloniki (up to a radius
  of 60 km) and Larissa, Patras, Herakleion, Volos, Lamia, Kalamata
  and Yannina (up to a radius of 25 km).
- Unfamiliar road signs and warnings, see p. 119.

WHAT TO SAY
[*For numbers, see p. 125*]

(Nine) litres of . . .	(Ἐννέα) λίτρα . . . (enneh-a) leetra . . .
(150) drachmas of . . .	(ἑκατό πενῆντα) δραχμές . . . (ek-at-o pen-eenda) thra-hmess . . .
standard	ἁπλή aplee
premium	σοῦπερ soopehr
diesel	ντῆζελ diesel
Fill it up, please	Νά τό γεμίσετε, παρακαλῶ na toh gemeesset-eh, parakalo
Will you check . . .	Μπορεῖτε νά κοιτάξετε . . . boreeteh na keetak-set-eh . . .
the oil	τό λάδι toh la-thee

the battery	τήν μπαταρία
	teen bataree-a
the radiator	τό ψυγείο
	toh pseeg-ee-o
the tyres	τά λάστιχα
	ta lastee-ha
I've run out of petrol	Ἔμεινα ἀπό πετρέλαιο
	em-eena apo petrel-eh-o
Can I borrow a can, please?	Μοῦ δανείζετε ἕνα δοχείο βενζίνης, παρακαλῶ;
	moo than-eezet-eh enna tho-hee-o venzeen-eess parakalo
My car has broken down	Χάλασε τό αὐτοκίνητο μου
	halasseh toh aftokeen-eeto moo
My car won't start	Τό αὐτοκίνητο μου δέν ξεκινάει
	toh aftokeen-eeto moo then ksek-eena-ee
I've had an accident	Εἶχα ἕνα ἀτύχημα
	ee-ha enna a-tee-heema
I've lost my car keys	Ἔχασα τά κλειδιά τοῦ αὐτοκινήτου μου
	eh-hassa ta kleeth-ya too aftokeen-eetoo moo
My car is ...	Τό αὐτοκίνητο μου εἶναι ...
	toh aftokeen-eeto moo eeneh ...
two kilometres away	δύο χιλιόμετρα ἀπό ἐδῶ
	thee-o heelee-ometra apo eth-o
three kilometres away	τρία χιλιόμετρα ἀπό ἐδῶ
	tree-a heelee-ometra apo eth-o
Can you help me, please?	Μπορεῖτε νά μέ βοηθήσετε, σᾶς παρακαλῶ;
	boreeteh na meh vo-eeth-eeset-eh sas parakalo
Do you do repairs?	Κάνετε ἐπισκευές;
	kan-et-eh ep-eeskev-ess
I have a puncture	Τρύπησε τό λάστιχο
	treepees-eh toh lastee-ho
I have a broken windscreen	Ἔσπασε τό μπροστινό τζάμι
	espas-eh toh brosteeno tzam-ee
I think the problem is here ... [point]	Νομίζω ὅτι τό πρόβλημα εἶναι ἐδῶ ...
	nomeezo otee toh prov-leema eeneh eth-o

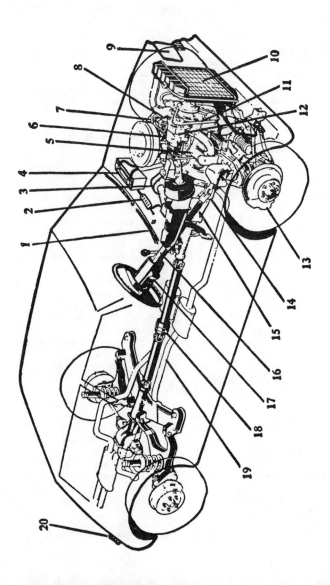

1 windscreen wipers	υαλοκαθαριστήρες ee-alok-athar-eesteer-ess
2 fuses	ασφάλεια asfalee-a
3 heater	καλοριφέρ kaloreef-ehr
4 battery	μπαταρία bataree-a
5 engine	μοτέρ motehr
6 fuel pump	αντλία βενζίνης antlee-a venzeen-eess
7 starter motor	στάρτερ startehr
8 carburettor	καρμπυρατέρ karbeera-tehr
9 lights	τα φώτα ta fota
10 radiator	ψυγείο pseeg-ee-o

11 fan belt	λουρί loo-ree
12 generator	γεννήτρια ghe-neetri-a
13 brakes	φρένα frenna
14 clutch	συμπλέκτης seeblek-teess
15 gear box	κιβώτιο ταχυτήτων keevot-yo ta-heeteeton
16 steering	τιμόνι teemon-ee
17 ignition	μίζα meeza
18 transmission	μετάδοση met-athoss-ee
19 exhaust	εξάτμιση eksat-meessee
20 indicators	φλας flass

I don't know what's wrong	Δέν ξέρω τί ἔχει
	then ksehr-o tee eh-hee
Can you . . .	Μπορειτε νά . . .
	boreeteh na . . .
repair the fault?	τό ἐπισκευάσετε;
	toh ep-eeskev-asset-eh
come and look?	ἔρθετε νά τό δεῖτε;
	ehr-thet-eh na toh theeteh
estimate the cost?	μοῦ πῆτε πόσο θά κάνει;
	moo peeteh posso tha kanee
write it down?	τό γράψετε;
	toh grapset-eh
Do you accept these coupons?	Δέχεστε αὐτά τά κουπόνια;
	theh-hess-teh afta ta koopon-ya
How long will the repair take?	Πόσο θά σᾶς πάρει νά τό
	ἐπισκευάσετε;
	posso tha sas par-ee na toh
	ep-eess-kehv-asset-eh
When will the car be ready?	Πότε θά εἶναι ἔτοιμο τό
	αὐτοκίνητο;
	pot-eh tha eeneh et-eemo toh
	aftokeen-eeto
Can I see the bill?	Μπορῶ νά δῶ τό λογαριασμό;
	boro na tho toh logaree-azmo
This is my insurance document	Ὁρίστε ἡ ἀσφάλεια μου
	oreesteh ee asfal-ya moo

HIRING A CAR

Can I hire a car?	Μπορῶ νά νοικιάσω ἕνα
	αὐτοκίνητο;
	boro na neek-yasso enna
	aftokeen-eeto
I need a car . . .	Θέλω ἕνα αὐτοκίνητο . . .
	thello enna aftokeen-eeto. . .
for two people	γιά δύο ἄτομα
	ya thee-o atoma
for five people	γιά πέντε ἄτομα
	ya pendeh atoma
for one day	γιά μία μέρα
	ya mee-a mehra
for five days	γιά πέντε μέρες
	ya pendeh mehress

for a week	γιά μία βδομάδα
	ya mee-a vthoma-tha
Can you write down . . .	Μοῦ γράφετε . . .
	moo graf-et-eh . . .
the deposit to pay?	τήν προκαταβολή;
	teen prokatavol-ee
the charge per kilometre?	πόσο κάνει τό χιλιόμετρο;
	posso kan-ee toh heelee-ometro
the daily charge?	πόσο κάνει τήν ἡμέρα;
	posso kan-ee teen eem-ehra
the cost of insurance?	πόσο κάνει ἡ ἀσφάλεια;
	posso kan-ee ee asfal-ya
Can I leave it (in Athens)?	Μπορῶ νά τό ἀφήσω (στήν Ἀθῆνα);
	boro na toh a-feeso (steen athee-na)
What documents do I need?	Τί ἔγγραφα χρειάζομαι;
	tee eng-rafa hree-az-om-eh

LIKELY REACTIONS

I don't do repairs	Δέν κάνω ἐπισκευές
	then kan-o ep-eeskev-ess
Where's your car?	Ποῦ εἶναι τό αὐτοκίνητο σας;
	poo eeneh toh aftokeen-eeto sas
What make is it?	Τί μάρκα εἶναι;
	tee marka eeneh
Come back tomorrow/on Monday	Ἐλᾶτε αὔριο/τή Δευτέρα
	ellat-eh avrio/tee thef-tehra

[For days of the week, see p. 129]

We don't hire cars	Δέν νοικιάζουμε αὐτοκίνητα
	then neek-yaz-oom-eh aftokeen-eeta
Your driving licence, please	Τήν ἄδεια ὁδηγήσεως, παρακαλῶ
	teen ath-ya o-thee-geesseh-oss parakalo
The mileage is unlimited	Δέν ὑπάρχει μίνιμουμ χιλιομετρικό ὅριο
	then eepar-hee minimum heelee-ometreek-o oree-o

Public transport

ESSENTIAL INFORMATION

- Finding the way to the bus station, a bus stop, a trolley stop, the railway station and a taxi stand, see p. 22.
- Remember that lining up for buses is not strictly followed.
- The railway network in Greece is not very extensive. The national railways connect Athens with the most important regions of the country. Buses are more frequent (much faster than trains).
- The underground in Athens is called 'Ο ΗΛΕΚΤΡΙΚΟΣ, and joins Piraeus with Athens and Kifissia.
- There are frequent ferry-boats to most islands from Piraeus.
- In Athens there are electric trolleys in addition to the bus services. For urban buses and trolleys there is a flat rate which you pay to the conductor. Some of these have no conductors, so no change is available and you drop the fare into a box. They have a large sign on the front: ΧΩΡΙΣ ΕΙΣΠΡΑΚΤΟΡΑ (without conductor) and you get in and pay at the front and get out at the back.
- Key words on signs: (see also p. 119)
  ΓΡΑΦΕΙΟΝ ΕΙΣΙΤΗΡΙΩΝ (ticket office)
  ΕΙΣΟΔΟΣ (entrance)
  ΑΠΑΓΟΡΕΥΕΤΑΙ Η ΕΙΣΟΔΟΣ (no entrance)
  ΑΝΟΔΟΣ (entrance, for buses)
  ΚΑΘΟΔΟΣ (exit, for buses)
  ΠΡΟΣ ΤΑΣ ΑΠΟΒΑΘΡΑΣ (to the platforms)
  ΓΡΑΦΕΙΟΝ ΠΛΗΡΟΦΟΡΙΩΝ (information office)
  ΟΣΕ (initials for Greek railways)
  ΚΤΕΛ (initials for Greek coach services)
  ΕΞΟΔΟΣ (exit)
  ΘΥΡΙΔΕΣ ΑΠΟΣΚΕΥΩΝ (left luggage)
  ΣΤΑΣΙΣ stop: in Athens the stops are yellow for trolleys and blue for buses. The sign shows a bus stop.
  ΔΡΟΜΟΛΟΓΙΟΝ
  (timetable)

WHAT TO SAY

Where does the ferry-boat for (Piraeus) leave from?	'Από ποῦ φεύγει τό φέρυ μπότ γιά τόν (Πειραιᾶ);
	apo poo fev-ghee toh ferry-boat ya ton (peereya)
At what time does the ferry-boat leave for (Piraeus)?	Τί ὥρα φεύγει τό φέρυ μπότ γιά τόν (Πειραιᾶ);
	tee ora fev-ghee toh ferry-boat ya ton (peereya)
At what time does the ferry-boat arrive in (Piraeus)?	Τί ὥρα φτάνει τό φέρυ μπότ στόν (Πειραιᾶ);
	tee ora ftan-ee toh ferry-boat ston (peereya)
Is this the ferry-boat for (Piraeus)?	Εἶναι αὐτό τό φερυ μπότ γιά τόν (Πειραιᾶ);
	eeneh afto toh ferry-boat ya ton (peereya)
Where does the bus for (Delphi) leave from?	'Από ποῦ φεύγει τό λεωφορεῖο γιά τούς (Δελφούς);
	apo poo fev-ghee toh leh-oforee-o ya tooss (thelfooss)
At what time does the bus leave for (Delphi)?	Τί ὥρα φεύγει τό λεωφορεῖο γιά τούς (Δελφούς);
	tee ora fev-ghee toh leh-oforee-o ya tooss (thelfooss)
At what time does the bus arrive at (Delphi)?	Τί ὥρα φτάνει τό λεωφορεῖο στούς (Δελφούς);
	tee ora ftan-ee toh leh-oforee-o stooss (thelfooss)
Is this the bus for (Delphi)?	Αὐτό εἶναι τό λεωφορεῖο γιά τούς (Δελφούς);
	afto eeneh toh leh-oforee-o ya tooss (thelfooss)
Do I have to change?	Πρέπει νά ἀλλάξω;
	prep-ee na allak-so
Where does . . . leave from?	'Από ποῦ φεύγει . . .
	apo poo fev-ghee
the bus	τό λεωφορεῖο;
	toh leh-oforee-o
the train	τό τραῖνο;
	toh tren-o
the underground	ὁ ἠλεκτρικός;
	o eelek-treekoss

Where does . . . leave from?	'Από πού φεύγει . . . apo poo fev-ghee . . .
the ferry-boat	τό φέρυ μπότ toh ferry-boat
for the airport	γιά τό ἀεροδρόμιο; ya toh ehr-othrom-yo
for the beach	γιά τήν παραλία; ya teen paralee-a
for the market place	γιά τήν ἀγορά; ya teen agorah
for the railway station	γιά τό σιδηροδρομικό σταθμό; ya toh see-theer-othrom-eeko stathmo
for the town centre	γιά τό κέντρο τῆς πόλης; ya toh kendro teess pol-eess
for St Dimitrios' church	γιά τόν Ἅγιο Δημήτριο; ya ton ag-yo thee-meetrio
for the swimming pool	γιά τήν πισίνα; ya teen pee-seena
Is this . . .	Αὐτό εἶναι . . . afto eeneh . . .
the bus for the market place?	τό λεωφορειο γιά τήν ἀγορά; toh leh-oforee-o ya teen agorah
the trolley for the railway station?	τό τρολλεϋ γιά τό σιδηροδρομικό σταθμό; toh trolley ya toh see-theer-othromeeko stathmo
Where can I get a taxi?	Πού μπορῶ νά βρῶ ἕνα ταξί; poo boro na vro enna taksee
Can you put me off at the right stop, please?	Μπορεῖτε νά μέ κατεβάσετε στή σωστή στάση, παρακαλῶ; boreeteh na meh kat-ev-asset-eh stee sostee stassee parakalo
Can I book a seat?	Μπορῶ νά κλείσω μιά θέση; boro na kleesso mee-a thessee
A single	Ἕνα ἁπλό εἰσιτήριο enna aplo eess-eeteerio
A return	Ἕνα εἰσιτήριο μετ'ἐπιστροφῆς enna eess-eeteerio met-ep-eestr-of-eess
First class	Πρώτη θέση prot-ee thess-ee

Second class	Δεύτερη θέση
	thef-tehree thessee
One adult	Ένας ενήλικας
	ennas en-eeleek-ass
Two adults	Δύο ενήλικες
	thee-o en-eeleek-ess
and one child	καί ένα παιδί
	keh enna peth-ee
and two children	καί δύο παιδιά
	keh thee-o peth-ya
How much is it?	Πόσο κάνει;
	posso kan-ee

LIKELY REACTIONS

Over there	Εκεί
	ek-ee
Here	Εδώ
	eth-o
Platform (1)	Πλατφόρμα νούμερο (ένα)
	platforma noomero (enna)
At (four o'clock)	Στίς (τέσσερεις)
[For times, see p. 127]	steess (tesser-eess)
Change at (Lamia)	Νά αλλάξετε στή (Λαμία)
	na allak-set-eh stee (lam-ee-a)
Change at (the town hall)	Νά αλλάξετε (στό Δημαρχείο)
	na allak-set-eh (sto theemar-hee-o)
This is your stop	Αυτή είναι ή στάση σας
	aftee eeneh ee stassee sas

Leisure

ESSENTIAL INFORMATION

- Finding the way to a place of entertainment, see p. 22.
- For times of day, see p. 127.
- Important signs, see p. 119.
- There are some resorts in Greece where you have to pay to go on the beach and to rent deckchairs and umbrellas.
- Smoking is forbidden in movies and theatres, but not in open-air cinemas, open during the summer months.
- You should tip movie and theatre usherettes who will also give you a programme.

WHAT TO SAY

At what time does . . . open?	Τί ὥρα ἀνοίγει . . .
	tee ora aneeg-ee . . .
the art gallery	ἡ πινακοθήκη;
	ee peenakoth-*ee*kee
the cinema	τό σινεμά;
	toh seenem*a*
the concert hall	ἡ αἴθουσα συναυλιῶν;
	ee *eth*-oossa seen-avlee-*o*n
the disco	ἡ ντισκοτέκ;
	ee discotheque
the museum	τό μουσεῖο;
	toh moossee-o
the nightclub	τό νάιτ κλάμπ;
	toh nightclub
the sports stadium	τό γήπεδο;
	toh y*ee*-petho
the swimming pool	ἡ πισίνα;
	ee pee-s-*ee*na
the theatre	τό θέατρο;
	toh th*eh*-atro
the zoo	ὁ ζωολογικός κῆπος;
	o zo-olog-*ee*koss k*ee*poss
At what time does . . . close?	Τί ὥρα κλείνει . . .
	tee ora kl*ee*nee . . .
the art gallery	ἡ πινακοθήκη;
[see above list]	ee peenakoth-*ee*kee

At what time does . . . start?	Τί ὥρα ἀρχίζει . . .
	tee ora ar-heezee . . .
the cabaret	τό καμπαρέ;
	toh cabaret
the concert	ἡ συναυλία;
	ee seen-avleea
the film	τό φίλμ;
	toh film
the match	τό μάτς;
	toh match
the play	τό θέατρο;
	toh theh-atro
the race	ὁ ἀγώνας;
	o agon-ass
How much is it . . .	Πόσο κάνει . . .
	posso kan-ee . . .
for an adult?	γιά τούς ἐνήλικες;
	ya tooss en-eeleek-ess
for a child?	γιά ἕνα παιδί;
	ya enna peth-ee
Two adults, please	Δύο ἐνήλικες, παρακαλῶ
	thee-o en-eeleek-ess parakalo
Three children, please	Τρία παιδιά, παρακαλῶ
[state price, if there's a choice]	tree-a peth-ya parakalo
Stalls/circle	Πλατεῖα/ἐξώστη
	plat-ee-a/ek-sostee
Do you have . . .	Ἔχετε . . .
	eh-het-eh. . .
a programme?	ἕνα πρόγραμμα;
	enna programma
a guide book?	ἕνα βιβλίο ὁδηγό;
	enna veevlee-o otheego
Where's the toilet please?	Ποῦ εἶναι ἡ τουαλέτα, παρακαλῶ;
	poo eeneh ee too-al-et-a parakalo
Where's the cloakroom?	Ποῦ εἶναι τό βεστιάριο;
	poo eeneh toh vestee-ario
I would like lessons in . . .	Θά ἤθελα μαθήματα . . .
	tha eeethella matheemata . . .
sailing	ἱστιοπλοΐας
	eestee-oplo-ee-ass
skiing	γιά σκί
	ya skee
sub-aqua diving	γιά ὑποβρύχιες βουτιές
	ya eepovree-hee-ess voot-ee-ess

I would like lessons in ...	Θά ἤθελα μαθήματα ... tha *eee*thella math*ee*mata ...
water skiing	γιά θαλάσσιο σκί ya thal*a*ss-yo sk*ee*
windsurfing	σέ ουιντσέρφιγκ seh windsurfing
Can I hire ...	Μπορῶ νά νοικιάσω ... bor*o* na neek-y*a*sso...
some skis	μερικά θαλάσσια σκί; mehr-eek*a* thal*a*ss-ya sk*ee*
a boat?	μία βάρκα; m*ee*-a v*a*rka
a fishing rod?	ἔνα καλάμι γιά ψάρεμα; enna kal*a*m-ee ya ps*a*rema
a deck-chair	μία ξαπλώστρα; m*ee*a ksap-l*o*stra
a sun umbrella?	μία τέντα γιά τόν ἥλιο; m*ee*-a t*e*nda ya ton *ee*l-yo
the necessary equipment?	τά ἀπαραίτητα ἐφόδια; ta apar*e*t-eeta ef-*o*thee-a
How much is it ...	Πόσο κάνει ... p*o*sso kan-ee ...
per day/per hour?	τή μέρα/τήν ὥρα; tee m*e*hra/teen *o*ra
Do I need a licence?	Χρειάζομαι ἄδεια; hree-*a*z-om-eh *a*th-ia

Asking if things are allowed

WHAT TO SAY

Excuse me, please	Μέ συγχωρεῖτε, παρακαλῶ meh seenhoreet-eh parakalo
May one . . . here?	'Επιτρέπεται . . . ἐδῶ; epeetrep-et-eh . . . etho
camp	ἡ κατασκήνωση katass-keenoss-ee
fish	τό ψάρεμα toh psarem-ah
park	τό παρκάρισμα toh parkareesmah
smoke	τό κάπνισμα toh kapneesmah
swim	τό κολύμπι toh koleembee
Can I . . .	Μπορο νά . . . bor-o na . . .
come in?	μπῶ ἐδῶ; boh etho
dance here?	χορέψω ἐδῶ; horepso etho
get a drink here?	πάρω ἕνα ποτό ἐδῶ; paro enna poto etho
get out this way?	βγῶ ἀπό ἐδῶ; vgoh apo etho
get something to eat here?	φάω ἐδῶ; fa-oh etho
leave my things here?	ἀφήσω τά πράγματα μου ἐδῶ; afeesso ta pragmata moo etho
look around?	ρίξω μία ματιά; reekso mee-a matya
sit here?	καθήσω ἐδῶ; katheesso etho
take photos here?	πάρω φωτογραφίες ἐδῶ; paro fotografeeyess etho
telephone here?	τηλεφωνήσω ἐδῶ; teelefoneessoh etho
wait here?	περιμένω ἐδῶ; pereemeno etho

LIKELY REACTIONS

Yes, certainly	Ναί, βεβαίως; neh vev-eh-oss
Help yourself	Βεβαίως vev-eh-oss
I think so	Μᾶλλον mallon
Of course	Φυσικά fee-seeka
Yes, but be careful	Ναί ἀλλά προσεκτικά neh alla pross-ek-teeka
No, certainly not	Ὄχι, δέν γίνεται o-hee then geenet-eh
I don't think so	Δέν νομίζω then nomeezo
Not normally	Συνήθως ὄχι seeneethoss o-hee
Sorry	Λυπᾶμαι leepam-eh

Reference

PUBLIC NOTICES

● Key words on signs for drivers, pedestrians, travellers, shoppers and overnight guests.

ΑΔΙΕΞΟΔΟΣ athee-*ek*-sothoss	Dead end
ΑΙΘΟΥΣΑ ΑΝΑΜΟΝΗΣ ethoossa anamon-*ees*s	Waiting room
ΑΝΑΜΕΙΝΑΤΕ anameenat-eh	Wait
ΑΝΑΧΩΡΗΣΕΙΣ ana-hor*ees*-eess	Departures
ΑΝΑΨΥΚΤΙΚΑ an-apseekteek-*a*	Refreshments
ΑΝΕΛΚΥΣΤΗΡ an-elkeest-*eer*	Lift
ΑΝΟΙΚΤΟΝ an-eekton	Open
ΑΝΔΡΩΝ anthr*on*	Gentlemen
ΑΠΑΓΟΡΕΥΕΤΑΙ apagor*ev*-et-eh	Forbidden
ΑΠΑΓΟΡΕΥΕΤΑΙ Η ΕΙΣΟΔΟΣ apagor*ev*-et-eh ee *ees*-othoss	No entry
ΑΠΑΓΟΡΕΥΕΤΑΙ Η ΣΤΑΘΜΕΥΣΙΣ apagor*ev*-et-eh ee stathmef-seess	No parking
ΑΠΑΓΟΡΕΥΕΤΑΙ ΤΟ ΚΑΠΝΙΣΜΑ apagor*ev*-et-eh toh *k*apnizma	No smoking
ΑΠΩΛΕΣΘΕΝΤΑ ΑΝΤΙΚΕΙΜΕΝΑ ap-ol-ess-thenda antik-*ee*mena	Lost property
ΑΡΓΑ arg*a*	Drive slowly
ΑΣΤΥΝΟΜΙΑ asteen-om*ee*-a	Police

ΑΦΙΞΕΙΣ afeek-seess	Arrivals
ΒΑΓΚΟΝ-ΡΕΣΤΩΡΑΝ vagon restoran	Dining car
ΓΡΑΦΕΙΟΝ ΕΚΔΟΣΕΩΣ ΕΙΣΙΤΗΡΙΩΝ grafee-on ek-thoss-eh-oss eess-eeteer-ee-on	Ticket office
ΓΡΑΦΕΙΟΝ ΠΛΗΡΟΦΟΡΙΩΝ grafee-on pleer-oforee-on	Information office
ΓΥΝΑΙΚΩΝ gheenek-on	Ladies
ΔΙΑΣΤΑΥΡΩΣΙΣ thee-astavross-eess	Crossroads
ΔΙΑ ΦΟΡΤΗΓΑ ΑΥΤΟΚΙΝΗΤΑ thee-a fort-eega aftokeen-eeta	For heavy vehicles
ΔΙΟΔΙΑ thee-oth-ya	Toll
ΕΘΝΙΚΗ ΟΔΟΣ ethneekee othoss	Highway
ΕΙΔΙΚΗ ΠΡΟΣΦΟΡΑ ee-theekee prosfora	Special offer
ΕΙΣΟΔΟΣ eess-othoss	Entrance
ΕΙΣΟΔΟΣ ΕΛΕΥΘΕΡΑ eess-othoss el-ef-thehra	Admission free
ΕΙΣΟΔΟΣ ΕΛΕΥΘΕΡΑ eess-oth-oss el-ef-thehra	Entrance free
ΕΚΠΤΩΣΕΙΣ ek-ptoss-eess	Sales
ΕΛΑΤΤΩΣΑΤΕ ΤΑΧΥΤΗΤΑ el-atossat-eh ta-heeteeta	Slow down
ΕΛΕΥΘΕΡΟΝ el-ef-thehron	Vacant
ΕΝΟΙΚΙΑΖΕΤΑΙ en-eek-yaz-et-eh	For hire
ΕΝΟΙΚΙΑΖΕΤΑΙ en-eek-yaz-et-eh	To let
ΕΝΟΙΚΙΑΖΟΝΤΑΙ ΔΩΜΑΤΙΑ eneekeeazondeh thomatee-a	Room for rent
ΕΞΟΔΟΣ ek-sothoss	Exit

ΙΣΟΠΕΔΟΣ ΔΙΑΒΑΣΙΣ eessopethoss thee-avass-eess	Level crossing
ΕΡΓΑ ΕΠΙ ΤΗΣ ΟΔΟΥ ehr-ga ep-ee teess othoo	Construction
ΕΞΟΔΟΣ ΚΙΝΔΥΝΟΥ ek-sothoss kintheenoo	Emergency exit
ΖΕΣΤΟ zesto	Hot (tap)
ΘΥΡΙΔΕΣ ΑΠΟΣΚΕΥΩΝ theer-eethess aposkev-on	Left luggage
ΙΔΙΩΤΙΚΟΝ ee-thee-oteekon	Private
ΚΑΤΕΙΛΗΜΜΕΝΟΝ kat-eeleemmen-on	Occupied
ΚΙΝΔΥΝΟΣ kinth-inoss	Danger
ΚΛΕΙΣΤΟΝ kleeston	Closed
ΚΡΥΟ kree-o	Cold
ΚΥΛΙΟΜΕΝΗ ΣΚΑΛΑ keel-yom-en-ee ska-la	Escalator
ΜΗ ΕΓΓΙΖΕΤΕ mee eng-eezet-eh	Do not touch
ΜΗ ΠΟΣΙΜΟ ΝΕΡΟ mee posseemo nehr-o	Not for drinking
ΜΟΝΟΔΡΟΜΟΣ monoth-romoss	One-way (street)
ΜΠΑΡ bar	Bar
ΝΟΣΟΚΟΜΕΙΟΝ noss-okomee-on	Hospital
ΟΔΗΓΟΣ othee-goss	Guide
ΟΙ ΠΑΡΑΒΑΤΑΙ ΘΑ ΔΙΩΧΘΟΥΝ ee paravat-eh tha thee-o-hthoon	Trespassers will be prosecuted
ΟΛΙΣΘΗΡΗ ΕΠΙΦΑΝΕΙΑ ol-eess-theeree ep-eefan-ya	Slippery surface (road)
ΟΡΙΟΝ ΤΑΧΥΤΗΤΟΣ oree-on ta-heeteetoss	Speed limit

ΟΡΟΦΟΣ (ΠΡΩΤΟΣ, ΔΕΥΤΕΡΟΣ, ΤΡΙΤΟΣ, ΕΙΣΟΓΕΙΟΝ, ΥΠΟΓΕΙΟΝ) orofoss (prot-oss, thefteross, treetoss, eessog-yon, eepog-yon)	Floor (first, second, third ground, basement)
ΠΕΖΟΙ pez-ee	Pedestrians
ΠΕΡΙΟΡΙΣΜΕΝΗ ΣΤΑΘΜΕΥΣΙΣ peri-oreezmen-ee stathmef-seess	Restricted parking
ΠΛΑΤΦΟΡΜΑ platforma	Platform
ΠΛΗΡΕΣ pleeress	No vacancies
ΠΟΡΕΙΑ ΥΠΟΧΡΕΩΤΙΚΗ ΔΕΞΙΑ poree-a eepo-hreh-oteekee theks-ya	Keep right
ΠΟΣΙΜΟ ΝΕΡΟ posseemo nehro	Drinking water
ΠΡΟΣΟΧΗ prosso-hee	Caution
ΠΡΟΣΟΧΗ ΣΚΥΛΟΣ prosso-hee skeeloss	Beware of the dog
ΠΡΟΣΟΧΗ ΣΤΑ ΤΡΑΙΝΑ prosso-hee sta tren-a	Beware of the trains
ΠΩΛΕΙΤΑΙ poleeteh	For sale
ΠΩΛΗΣΙΣ pol-eess-eess	Sale
ΡΕΣΕΠΣΙΟΝ ressepsee-on	Reception
ΣΕΛΦ-ΣΕΡΒΙΣ self-service	Self-service
ΣΤΑΘΜΕΥΣΙΣ ΑΥΤΟΚΙΝΗΤΩΝ stathmef-seess aftokeen-eeton	Car park
ΣΥΡΑΤΕ seerat-eh	Push

ΣΧΟΛΕΙΟΝ skol*ee*-on	School
TAMEION tam-*ee*-on	Cash desk
ΤΕΛΩΝΕΙΟΝ tel-on*ee*-on	Customs
ΤΟΥΑΛΕΤΑ too-al-*et*-a	Bathroom
ΤΡΑΠΕΖΑΡΙΑ trap-ez-ar*ee*-a	Dining room
ΦΑΝΑΡΙΑ fan*a*r-ee-a	Traffic lights
ΩΘΗΣΑΤΕ o*thee*-sat-eh	Pull

ABBREVIATIONS

Ἅγ.	Ἅγιος	Saint
ΑΠ	Ἀστυνομία Πόλεων	Municipal Police
ἀρ.	ἀριθμός	street number
ΔΕΗ	Δημόσια Ἐπιχείρησις Ἠλεκτρισμοῦ	Electric Company of Greece
δηλ.	δηλαδή	that is to say
Δίς	Δεσποινίς	Miss
δολλ.	δολλάρια	dollars
δρχ.	δραχμές	drachmas
Δσις	Διεύθυνσις	manager
ΕΕΣ	Ἑλληνικός Ἐρυθρός Σταυρός	Greek Red Cross
ἐθν.	ἐθνικός	national
ἑκ.	ἑκατοστά	centimetres
	ἑκατομμύρια	millions
Ἑλλ.	Ἑλληνικός	Greek
ΕΛΠΑ	Ἑλληνική Λέσχη Περιηγήσεων καὶ Αὐτοκινήτου	Automobile and Touring Club of Greece
ΕΛ.ΤΑ.	Ἑλληνικά Ταχυδρομεῖα	Greek Post Office
ΕΟΤ	Ἑλληνικός Ὀργανισμός Τουρισμοῦ	Greek Tourist Organization
ΙΚΑ	Ἵδρυμα Κοινωνικῶν Ἀσφαλίσεων	National Health Insurance
Κ./Κος	Κύριος	Mr
Κα	Κυρία	Mrs
κλπ.	καί τά λοιπά	etc.
Λεωφ.	Λεωφόρος	avenue
λογ/μος	λογαριασμός	bill
λ.στ.	λίραι στερλίναι	sterling pounds
μ.μ.	μετά μεσηβρίαν	p.m.
μ.Χ.	μετά Χριστόν	AD
Ὁδ.	Ὁδός	street
ΟΣΕ	Ὀργανισμός Σιδηροδρόμων Ἑλλάδος	Railway Company of Greece
ΟΤΕ	Ὀργανισμός Τηλεπικοινωνιῶν Ἑλλάδος	Telecommunications Company of Greece
π.μ.	πρό μεσηβρίας	a.m.
π.Χ.	πρό Χριστοῦ	BC
π.χ.	παραδείγματος χάριν	for example
ΤΑ	Τουριστική Ἀστυνομία	Tourist Police
τηλ.	τηλέφωνο	telephone
χλμ.	χιλιόμετρα	kilometres

NUMBERS

Cardinal numbers

0	μηδέν	meethen
1	ἕνας, μία, ἕνα	ennas mee-a enna
2	δύο	thee-o
3	τρία	tree-a
4	τέσσερα	tessera
5	πέντε	pendeh
6	ἕξη	eksee
7	ἑπτά	epta
8	ὀκτώ	okto
9	ἐννέα	enneh-a
10	δέκα	theh-ka
11	ἕντεκα	endek-a
12	δώδεκα	thothek-a
13	δεκατρία	thek-atree-a
14	δεκατέσσερα	thek-atesser-a
15	δεκαπέντε	thek-apendeh
16	δεκαέξη	theh-ka-eksee
17	δεκαεπτά	theh-ka-ept-a
18	δεκαοκτώ	theh-ka-okto
19	δεκαεννέα	theh-ka-enneh-a
20	εἴκοσι	eekossee
21	εἴκοσι ἕνα	eekossee enna
22	εἴκοσι δύο	eekossee thee-o
23	εἴκοσι τρία	eekossee tree-a
24	εἴκοσι τέσσερα	eekossee tessera
25	εἴκοσι πέντε	eekossee pendeh
26	εἴκοσι ἕξη	eekossee eksee
27	εἴκοσι ἑπτά	eekossee epta
28	εἴκοσι ὀκτώ	eekossee okto
29	εἴκοσι ἐννέα	eekossee enneh-a
30	τριάντα	tree-anda
35	τριάντα πέντε	tree-anda pendeh
38	τριάντα ὀκτώ	tree-anda okto
40	σαράντα	saranda
41	σαράντα ἕνα	saranda enna
45	σαράντα πέντε	saranda pendeh
48	σαράντα ὀκτώ	saranda okto
50	πενῆντα	pen-eenda
55	πενῆντα πέντε	pen-eenda pendeh
56	πενῆντα ἕξη	pen-eenda eksee

60	ἑξήντα	ekseenda
65	ἑξήντα πέντε	ekseenda pendeh
70	ἑβδομήντα	ev-thomeenda
75	ἑβδομήντα πέντε	ev-thomeenda pendeh
80	ὀγδόντα	ogthonda
85	ὀγδόντα πέντε	ogthonda pendeh
90	ἐνενήντα	enneh-neenda
95	ἐνενήντα πέντε	enneh-neenda pendeh
100	ἑκατό	ek-at-o
101	ἑκατόν ἕνα	ek-at-on enna
102	ἑκατόν δύο	ek-at-on thee-o
125	ἑκατόν εἴκοσι πέντε	ek-at-on eekossee pendeh
150	ἑκατόν πενήντα	ek-at-on pen-eenda
175	ἑκατόν ἑβδομήντα πέντε	ek-at-on ev-thomeenda pendeh
200	διακόσια	thee-akoss-ya
300	τριακόσια	tree-akoss-ya
400	τετρακόσια	tetra-koss-ya
500	πεντακόσια	pend-akoss-ya
1,000	χίλια	heel-ya
1,500	χίλια πεντακόσια	heel-ya pend-akoss-ya
2,000	δύο χιλιάδες	thee-o heel-yathess
5,000	πέντε χιλιάδες	pendeh heel-yathess
10,000	δέκα χιλιάδες	theh-ka heel-yathess
100,000	ἑκατόν χιλιάδες	ek-at-on heel-yathess
1,000,000	ἕνα ἑκατομμύριο	enna ekatomeereeo

Ordinal numbers

1st	πρῶτος, πρώτη, πρῶτο (1ος)	prot-oss prot-ee prot-o
2nd	δεύτερος (2ος)	thefteross
3rd	τρίτος (3ος)	treetoss
4th	τέταρτος (4ος)	tet-artoss
5th	πέμπτος (5ος)	pemp-toss
6th	ἕκτος (6ος)	ektoss
7th	ἕβδομος (7ος)	ev-thom-oss
8th	ὄγδοος (8ος)	ogtho-oss
9th	ἔννατος (9ος)	ennat-oss
10th	δέκατος (10ος)	thek-at-oss
11th	ἐντέκατος (11ος)	endeka-toss
12th	δωδέκατος (12ος)	tho-theka-toss

TIME

What time is it?	Τί ὥρα εἶναι; tee ora eeneh
It's ...	Εἶναι ... eeneh ...
one o'clock	μία mee-a
two o'clock	δύο thee-o
three o'clock	τρεῖς treess
four o'clock	τέσσερες tesser-ess
in the morning	τό πρωί toh pro-ee
in the afternoon	τό ἀπόγευμα toh apog-evma
in the evening	τό βράδυ toh vrath-ee
at night	τή νύχτα tee neeh-tah
It's ...	Εἶναι ... eeneh ...
noon	μεσημέρι mess-eemehree
midnight	μεσάνυχτα messan-ee-hta
It's ...	Εἶναι ... eeneh ...
five past five	πέντε καί πέντε pendeh keh pendeh
ten past five	πέντε καί δέκα pendeh keh theh-ka
a quarter past five	πέντε καί τέταρτο pendeh keh tet-arto·
twenty past five	πέντε καί εἴκοσι pendeh keh eekossee
twenty-five past five	πέντε καί εἴκοσι πέντε pendeh keh eekossee pendeh
half past five	πέντε καί μισή pendeh keh meessee

It's . . .	Είναι . . .
	eeneh . . .
twenty-five to six	έξη παρά είκοσι πέντε
	eksee para eekossee pendeh
twenty to six	έξη παρά είκοσι
	eksee para eekossee
a quarter to six	έξη παρά τέταρτο
	eksee para tet-arto
ten to six	έξη παρά δέκα
	eksee para theh-ka
five to six	έξη παρά πέντε
	eksee para pendeh
At what time . . . (does the train leave)?	Τί ώρα (φεύγει τό τραίνο);
	tee ora (fev-ghee toh tren-o)
At . . .	Στίς . . .
	steess . . .
13.00	δέκα τρείς
	theh-ka treess
14.05	δέκα τέσσερες καί πέντε
	theh-ka tesser-ess keh pendeh
15.10	δέκα πέντε καί δέκα
	theh-ka pendeh keh theh-ka
16.15	δέκα έξη καί δέκα πέντε
	theh-ka eksee keh theh-ka pendeh
17.20	δέκα έπτά καί είκοσι
	theh-ka epta keh eekossee
18.25	δέκα όκτώ καί είκοσι πέντε
	theh-ka okto keh eekossee pendeh
19.30	δέκα έννέα καί τριάντα
	theh-ka ennea keh tree-and-a
20.35	είκοσι καί τριάντα πέντε
	eekossee keh tree-anda pendeh
21.40	είκοσι μία καί σαράντα
	eekossee mee-a keh saranda
22.45	είκοσι δύο καί σαράντα πέντε
	eekossee thee-o keh saranda pendeh
23.50	είκοσι τρείς καί πενήντα
	eekossee treess keh pen-eenda
00.55	δώδεκα καί πενήντα πέντε
	thoth-eka keh pen-eenda pendeh
in ten minutes	σέ δέκα λεπτά
	seh theh-ka lepta

in a quarter of an hour	σέ ἕνα τέταρτο
	seh enna tet-arto
in half an hour	σέ μισή ὥρα
	seh meessee ora
in three quarters of an hour	σέ τρία τέταρτα
	seh tree-a tet-arta

DAYS

Monday	Δευτέρα
	thef-tehra
Tuesday	Τρίτη
	treetee
Wednesday	Τετάρτη
	tet-artee
Thursday	Πέμπτη
	pemp-tee
Friday	Παρασκευή
	paraskev-ee
Saturday	Σάββατο
	savvato
Sunday	Κυριακή
	keeree-ak-ee
last Monday	τήν προηγούμενη Δευτέρα
	teen pro-eegoomen-ee thef-tehra
next Tuesday	τήν ἐπόμενη Τρίτη
	teen ep-om-en-ee treetee
on Wednesday	τήν Τετάρτη
	teen tet-artee
on Thursdays	κάθε Πέμπτη
	kath-eh pemp-tee
until Friday	μέχρι τήν Παρασκευή
	meh-hree teen paraskev-ee
before Saturday	πρίν τό Σάββατο
	preen toh savvato
after Sunday	μετά τήν Κυριακή
	meta teen keeree-ak-ee
the day before yesterday	προχθές
	pro-hthess
two days ago	πρίν δύο μέρες
	preen thee-o mehr-ess
yesterday	χθές
	hthess

yesterday morning	χθές τό πρωί
	hthess toh pro-*ee*
yesterday afternoon	χθές τό ἀπόγευμα
	hthess toh ap*og*-evma
last night	χθές τό βράδυ
	hthess toh vrath-ee
today	σήμερα
	seemera
this morning	τό πρωί
	toh pro-*ee*
this afternoon	τό ἀπόγευμα
	toh ap*og*-evma
tonight	τό βράδυ
	toh vrath-ee
tomorrow	αὔριο
	avrio
tomorrow morning	αὔριο τό πρωί
	avrio toh pro-*ee*
tomorrow afternoon	αὔριο τό ἀπόγευμα
	avrio toh ap*og*-evma
tomorrow evening	αὔριο βράδυ
	avrio vrath-ee
tomorrow night	αὔριο βράδυ
	avrio vrath-ee
the day after tomorrow	μεθαύριο
	methavrio

MONTHS AND DATES

January	Ἰανουάριος
	yanoo-*ar*-ee-oss
February	Φεβρουάριος
	fevroo-*ar*-ee-oss
March	Μάρτιος
	*mar*tee-oss
April	Ἀπρίλιος
	ap*ree*lee-oss
May	Μάϊος
	ma-ee-oss
June	Ἰούνιος
	ee-*oo*nee-oss
July	Ἰούλιος
	ee-*oo*lee-oss
August	Αὔγουστος
	*a*vgoost-oss
September	Σεπτέμβριος
	sep*tem*-vree-oss
October	Ὀκτώβριος
	ok*to*vree-oss
November	Νοέμβριος
	no-*em*-vree-oss
December	Δεκέμβριος
	thek-*em*-vree-oss
in January	τόν Ἰανουάριο
	ton yanoo-*ar*-ee-o
until February	μέχρι τόν φεβρουάριο
	meh-hree ton fev-roo-*ar*-ee-o
before March	πρίν τόν Μάρτιο
	preen ton *mar*tee-o
after April	μετά τόν Ἀπρίλιο
	met-*a* ton ap*ree*lee-o
during May	κατά τήν διάρκεια τοῦ Μαΐου
	kata *teen* thee-*ark*-ya too ma-*ee*-oo
not until June	ὄχι πρίν τόν Ἰούνιο
	o-hee preen ton ee-*oo*nee-o
the beginning of July	ἀρχές Ἰουλίου
	ar-hess ee-oo*lee*-oo
the middle of August	μέσα Αὐγούστου
	messa avg*oo*st-oo

the end of September	τέλη Σεπτεμβρίου
	tel-ee septem-vree-oo
last month	τόν προηγούμενο μήνα
	ton pro-eegoomen-o meena
this month	αὐτό τό μήνα
	afto toh meena
next month	τόν ἐπόμενο μήνα
	ton ep-om-en-o meena
in spring	τήν ἄνοιξη
	teen an-eeksee
in summer	τό καλοκαίρι
	toh kalok-ehree
in autumn	τό φθινόπωρο
	toh ftheen-op-oro
in winter	τό χειμώνα
	toh heemona
this year	αὐτό τό χρόνο
	afto toh hron-o
last year	πέρυσι
	pehr-eessee
next year	τοῦ χρόνου
	too hron-oo
in 1983	τό χίλια ἐννιακόσια ὀγδόντα τρία
	toh heel-ya enneh-akoss-ya ogthonda tree-a
in 1985	τό χίλια ἐννιακόσια ὀγδόντα πέντε
	toh heel-ya enneh-akoss-ya ogthonda pendeh
in 1990	τό χίλια ἐννιακόσια ἐνενήντα
	toh heel-ya enneh-akoss-ya enneneenda
What's the date today?	Πόσο ἔχει ὁ μῆνας σήμερα;
	posso eh-hee o meen-ass seemera
It's the 6th of March	Εἶναι ἔξη Μαρτίου
	eeneh eksee martee-oo
It's the 12th April	Εἶναι δώδεκα Ἀπριλίου
	eeneh thoth-eka apreelee-oo
It's the 21st of August	Εἶναι εἴκοσι μία Αὐγούστου
	eeneh eekossee mee-a avgoost-oo

Public holidays

● On these days offices, shops and schools are closed:

1 January	Πρωτοχρονιά	New Year's Day
6 January	Ἐπιφάνεια	Epiphany
	Καθαρή Δευτέρα	Clean Monday: beginning of Lent
moveable dates	Μεγάλη Παρασκευή	Good Friday
	Δεύτερη μέρα τοῦ Πάσχα	Easter Monday
	Πεντηκοστή	Whit Monday
25 March	25 Μαρτίου	Independence Day
1 May	Πρωτομαγιά	May Day
15 August	15 Αὐγούστου	Assumption
28 October	28 Ὀκτωβρίου	Ochi Day
25 December	Χριστούγεννα	Christmas Day
26 December	Δεύτερη μέρα τῶν Χριστουγέννων	Boxing Day

COUNTRIES AND NATIONALITIES
Countries

Australia	Αὐστραλία
	afstral*ee*-a
for Australia	Γιά τήν Αὐστραλία
	ya teen afstral*ee*-a
to Australia	Στήν Αὐστραλία
	steen afstral*ee*-**a**
Austria	Αὐστρία
	afstr*ee*-a
Belgium	Βέλγιο
	v*e*lg-yo
for Belgium	Γιά τό Βέλγιο
	ya toh v*e*lg-yo
to Belgium	Στό Βέλγιο
	sto v*e*lg-yo
Britain	Βρετανvία
	vret-ann*ee*-**a**
Canada	Καναδᾶς
	kana-th*a*ss
for Canada	Γιά τόν Καναδᾶ
	y*a* ton kana-th*a*
to Canada	Στόν Καναδᾶ
	ston kana-th*a*
East African	'Ανατολική Ἀφρική
	anatoleek*ee* afreek*ee*
Eire	'Ιρλανδία
	eerlan-th*ee*-**a**
England	'Αγγλία
	angl*ee*-a
France	Γαλλία
	gall-*ee*a
Greece	'Ελλάδα
	ell*a*tha
India	'Ινδία
	een-th*ee*-a
Italy	'Ιταλία
	eetal-*ee*-a
Luxembourg	Λουξεμβοῦργο
	looksemv*oo*rgo

Netherlands	Ὀλλανδία
	ollan-th*ee*-a
New Zealand	Νέα Ζηλανδία
	neh-a zeelan-th*ee*-a
Northern Ireland	Βόρειος Ἰρλανδία
	voree-oss eerlan-th*ee*-a
Pakistan	Πακιστάν
	pakist*a*n
Portugal	Πορτογαλία
	portogal-*ee*-a
Scotland	Σκωτία
	skot-*ee*-a
South African	Νότιος Ἀφρική
	notee-oss afreek*ee*
Spain	Ἰσπανία
	eespan-*ee*-a
Switzerland	Ἐλβετία
	elvet-*ee*-a
United States	Οἱ Ἡνωμένες Πολιτεῖες
	ee eenomen-ess poleet*ee*-ess
Wales	Οὐαλλία
	oo-al-l*ee*-a
West Germany	Δυτική Γερμανία
	theeteek-*ee* yehr-man*ee*-a
West Indies	Οἱ Δυτικές Ἰνδίες
	ee theeteek-ess een-th*ee*-ess
for the West Indies	Γιά τίς Δυτικές Ἰνδίες
	ya teess theeteek-ess een-th*ee*-ess
to the West Indies	Στίς Δυτικές Ἰνδίες
	steess theeteek-ess een-th*ee*-ess

Nationalities
(Use the first alternative for men, the second for women)

American	'Αμερικανός/'Αμερικανίδα
	amerikan-*oss*/amerikan-*eetha*
Australian	Αὐστραλός/Αὐστραλέζα
	afstral-*oss*/afstral-*ez-a*
British	Βρεταννός/Βρεταννίδα
	vretann-*oss*/vrettan-*eetha*
Canadian	Καναδός/Καναδέζα
	kanath-*oss*/kanath*ez-a*
East African	ἀπό τήν 'Ανατολική 'Αφρική
	ap*o* teen anatoleek*ee* afreek*ee*
English	'Εγγλέζος/'Εγγλέζα
	engl*ez-oss*/engl*ez-a*
Indian	'Ινδός/'Ινδή
	eenth*oss*/eenth*ee*
Irish	'Ιρλανδός/'Ιρλανδή
	eerlan-th*oss*/eerlan-th*ee*
a New Zealander	Νέο Ζηλανδός/Νέο Ζηλανδή
	neh-ozeelan-th*oss*/neh-ozeelan-th*ee*
a Pakistani	Πακιστανός/Πακιστανή
	pakistan-*oss*/pakistan-*ee*
Scots	Σκωτσέζος/Σκωτσέζα
	skots*ez-oss*/skots*ez-a*
South African	ἀπό τήν Νότια 'Αφρική
	ap*o* teen n*o*tee-a afreek*ee*
Welsh	Οὐαλλός/Οὐαλλή
	oo-al-l*oss*/oo-al-l*ee*
West Indian	ἀπό τίς Δυτικές 'Ινδίες
	ap*o* teess theeteek-*ess* eenth*ee-ess*

DEPARTMENT STORE GUIDE

ΑΝΔΡΙΚΑ ΕΙΔΗ	Menswear
ΑΝΔΡΙΚΑ ΕΣΩΡΟΥΧΑ	Underclothes
ΑΡΩΜΑΤΟΠΩΛΕΙΟΝ	Perfumery
ΓΡΑΒΑΤΕΣ	Ties
ΓΥΝΑΙΚΕΙΑ ΕΙΔΗ	Ladies' fashion
ΓΥΝΑΙΚΕΙΑ ΕΣΩΡΟΥΧΑ	Lingerie
ΓΥΝΑΙΚΕΙΙΑ ΕΣΩΡΟΥΧΑ	Underwear (women)
ΔΕΡΜΑΤΙΝΑ ΕΙΔΗ	Leather goods
ΔΕΥΤΕΡΟΣ	Second
ΔΙΣΚΟΙ	Records
ΔΩΡΑ	Presents
ΕΙΔΗ ΚΑΘΑΡΙΣΜΟΥ	Cleaning material
ΕΙΔΗ ΚΑΤΑΣΚΗΝΩΣΕΩΣ	Camping
ΕΙΔΗ ΚΡΕΒΒΑΤΟΚΑΜΑΡΑΣ	Bedding
ΕΙΔΗ ΡΑΠΤΙΚΗΣ	Haberdashery
ΕΠΙΠΛΑ	Furniture
ΕΠΙΠΛΑ ΚΟΥΖΙΝΑΣ	Kitchen furniture
ΕΤΟΙΜΑ ΕΝΔΥΜΑΤΑ	Ready made clothing
ΖΩΝΕΣ	Belts
ΗΛΕΚΤΡΙΚΑ ΕΙΔΗ	Electrical appliances
ΚΑΛΛΥΝΤΙΚΑ	Cosmetics
ΚΑΛΤΣΕΣ	Stockings
ΚΟΣΜΗΜΑΤΑ	Jewellery
ΚΟΥΒΕΡΤΕΣ	Blankets
ΚΟΥΡΤΙΝΕΣ	Curtains
ΜΑΞΙΛΑΡΙΑ	Cushions
ΜΠΛΟΥΖΕΣ	Blouses
ΟΡΟΦΟΣ	Floor
ΠΑΙΔΙΚΑ	Children
ΠΑΙΧΝΙΔΙΑ	Toys
ΠΑΝΤΟΦΛΕΣ	Slippers
ΠΗΛΙΝΑ ΕΙΔΗ	Earthenware
ΠΗΛΙΝΑ ΣΚΕΥΗ	Crockery
ΠΛΗΡΟΦΟΡΙΕΣ	Information
ΠΟΡΣΕΛΛΑΝΕΣ	China
ΠΟΥΛΟΒΕΡ	Pullovers
ΠΡΩΤΟΣ	First
ΛΕΥΚΑ ΕΙΔΗ	Linen
ΣΙΔΗΡΙΚΑ	Hardware
ΣΤΗΘΟΔΕΣΜΟΙ	Bras

ΤΑΜΕΙΟΝ	Accounts
ΤΑΞΕΙΔΙΩΤΙΚΑ ΕΙΔΗ	Travel articles
ΤΑΠΕΤΣΑΡΙΑΙ	Furnishing fabrics
ΤΕΤΑΡΤΟΣ	Fourth
ΤΡΙΤΟΣ	Third
ΤΡΟΦΙΜΑ	Food
ΥΑΛΙΚΑ ΕΙΔΗ	Glassware
ΥΠΟΓΕΙΟΝ	Basement
ΥΠΟΚΑΜΙΣΑ	Shirts
ΥΦΑΣΜΑΤΑ	Drapery
ΦΩΤΟΓΡΑΦΙΚΑ ΕΙΔΗ	Photography
ΧΑΛΙΑ	Carpets
ΧΑΡΤΙΚΑ	Stationery

CONVERSION TABLES

Read the centre column of these tables from right to left to convert
from metric to imperial and from left to right to convert from
imperial to metric e.g. 5 litres = 8.80 pints; 5 pints = 2.84 litres

pints		litres		gallons		litres
1.76	1	0.57		0.22	1	4.55
3.52	2	1.14		0.44	2	9.09
5.28	3	1.70		0.66	3	13.64
7.07	4	2.27		0.88	4	18.18
8.80	5	2.84		1.00	5	22.73
10.56	6	3.41		1.32	6	27.28
12.32	7	3.98		1.54	7	31.82
14.08	8	4.55		1.76	8	36.37
15.84	9	5.11		1.98	9	40.91

ounces		grams		pounds		kilos
0.04	1	28.35		2.20	1	0.45
0.07	2	56.70		4.41	2	0.91
0.11	3	85.05		6.61	3	1.36
0.14	4	113.40		8.82	4	1.81
0.18	5	141.75		11.02	5	2.27
0.21	6	170.10		13.23	6	2.72
0.25	7	198.45		15.43	7	3.18
0.28	8	226.80		17.64	8	3.63
0.32	9	255.15		19.84	9	4.08

inches		centimetres		yards		metres
0.39	1	2.54		1.09	1	0.91
0.79	2	5.08		2.19	2	1.83
1.18	3	7.62		3.28	3	2.74
1.58	4	10.16		4.37	4	3.66
1.95	5	12.70		5.47	5	4.57
2.36	6	15.24		6.56	6	5.49
2.76	7	17.78		7.66	7	6.40
3.15	8	20.32		8.65	8	7.32
3.54	9	22.86		9.84	9	8.23

miles		kilometres
0.62	1	1.61
1.24	2	3.22
1.86	3	4.83
2.49	4	6.44
3.11	5	8.05
3.73	6	9.66
4.35	7	11.27
4.97	8	12.87
5.59	9	14.48

A quick way to convert kilometres to miles: divide by 8 and multiply by 5. To convert miles to kilometres: divide by 5 and multiply by 8.

fahrenheit (°F)	centigrade (°C)		lbs/ sq in	k/ sq cm
212°	100°	boiling point	18	1.3
100°	38°		20	1.4
98.4°	36.9°	body temperature	22	1.5
86°	30°		25	1.7
77°	25°		29	2.0
68°	20°		32	2.3
59°	15°		35	2.5
50°	10°		36	2.5
41°	5°		39	2.7
32°	0°	freezing point	40	2.8
14°	−10°		43	3.0
−4°	−20°		45	3.2
			46	3.2
			50	3.5
			60	4.2

To convert °C to °F, divide by 5, multiply by 9 and add 32. To convert °F to °C, take away 32, divide by 9 and multiply by 5.

CLOTHING SIZES

Remember – always try on clothes before buying. Clothing sizes are usually unreliable.

Women's dresses and suits

Europe	38	40	42	44	46	48
UK	32	34	36	38	40	42
USA	10	12	14	16	18	20

Men's suits and coats

Europe	46	48	50	52	54	56
UK and USA	36	38	40	42	44	46

Men's shirts

Europe	36	37	38	39	41	42	43
UK and USA	14	14½	15	15½	16	16½	17

Socks

Europe	38–39	39–40	40–41	41–42	42–43
UK and USA	9½	10	10½	11	11½

Shoes

Europe	34	35½	36½	38	39	41	42	43	44	45
UK	2	3	4	5	6	7	8	9	10	11
USA	3½	4½	5½	6½	7½	8½	9½	10½	11½	12½

Do it yourself

Some notes on the language

This section does not deal with 'grammar' as such. The purpose here is to explain some of the most obvious and elementary nuts and bolts of the language, based on the principle phrases included in the book. This information should enable you to produce numerous sentences of your own making, although you will obviously still be fairly limited in what you can say.

THE

All nouns in Greek belong to one of three genders: masculine, feminine or neuter; this includes inanimate objects as well as living beings (see table opposite).

Important things to remember

● In the word list, *the* in the singular is:
  ό (o) before masculine nouns
  ή (ee) before feminine nouns
  τό (toh) before neuter nouns
● You can often tell if a noun is masculine, feminine or neuter by its ending. Most masculine nouns in the singular end in -ος (oss). Some end in -ας (ass) or -ης (eess) but there are few examples in the phrase book. Most feminine nouns in -η (ee) or -α (ah) and most neuter nouns in -o (oh), or ι (ee). If you are reading a word with ό (o), ή (ee), τό (toh) in front of it, you can detect its gender immediately: ό κατάλογος (o katalogoss) is masculine (m. in dictionaries), ή θαλίτσα (ee valeetsa) is feminine (f. in dictionaries) and τό δωμάτιο (toh thomateeo) is neuter (n. in dictionaries).
● Does it matter? Not unless you want to make a serious attempt to speak correctly and scratch beneath the surface of the language. You would be understood, if you said ή κατάλογος (ee katalogoss) or ό δρομολόγιο (o thromologeeo) providing your pronunciation was reasonable and you stressed the word in the right place.

The (singular)	masculine	feminine	neuter
the address		ή διεύθυνση ee thee- eftheensee	
the apple			τό μῆλο toh meeloh
the bill	ό λογαριασμός o logareeasmoss		
the cup of tea			τό τσάϊ toh tsaee
the glass of beer		ή μπύρα ee beera	
the key			τό κλειδί toh kleethee
the menu	ό κατάλογος o katalogoss		
the newspaper		ή 'εφημερίδα ee efeemereetha	
the receipt		ή ἀπόδειξη ee apotheeksee	
the sandwich			τό σάντουϊτς toh sandwich
the suitcase		ή βαλίτσα ee valeetsa	

the telephone
  directory
	ό τηλεφωνικός
	  κατάλογος
	o teelefoneekoss
	  katalogoss		

the timetable			τό δρομολόγιο toh thromologeeo

In phrases beginning: 'Have you got the . . .?'
'I'd like the . . .?'
'Where can I get the . . .?'

Greek nouns and articles become the object of the sentence and change to form the accusative. In the singular that means:

	the	noun endings
masculine	ὁ (o) becomes τό (toh)	-ος (oss) becomes -ο (oh)
feminine	ἡ (ee) becomes τή (tee)	no change
neuter	no change	no change

e.g. ὁ κατάλογος (o katalogoss) becomes τό κατάλογο (toh katalogo) and ἡ βαλίτσα (ee valeetsa) becomes τή βαλίτσα (tee valeetsa).

Practise saying and writing these sentences in Greek (masculine nouns are marked * to remind you that *both* the article and the noun ending change, but remember to change the article with feminine nouns). When you have understood the sentences, we suggest that you cover up the Greek and try yourself to work out translations.

Have you got the suitcase?	Ἔχετε τή βαλίτσα; eheteh tee valeetsa
Have you got the key?.	Ἔχετε τό κλειδί eheteh toh kleethee;
*Have you got the menu?	Ἔχετε τό κατάλογο; eheteh toh katalogo
I'd like the key	Θά ἤθελα τό κλειδί; tha eethela toh kleethee
I'd like the timetable	Θά ἤθελα τό δρομολόγιο tha eethela toh thromologeeo
*I'd like the bill	Θά ἤθελα τό λογαριασμό tha eethela toh logareeasmoh
I'd like the receipt	Θά ἤθελα τήν ἀπόδειξη tha eethela teen apotheeksee
Where can I get the key?	Ποῦ μπορῶ νά βρῶ τό κλειδί; poo boro na vro toh kleethee
Where can I get the suitcase?	Ποῦ μπορῶ νά βρῶ τή βαλίτσα; poo boro na vro tee valeetsa
Where can I get the address?	Ποῦ μπορῶ νά βρῶ τή διεύθυνση; poo boro na vro tee thee-eftheensee

Try adding 'please': παρακαλῶ (parakalo)

The (plural)	masculine	feminine	neuter
the addresses		οἱ διευθύνσεις ee thee-eftheensees	
the apples			τά μῆλα ta meela
the·baggage			τά πράγματα ta pragmata
the bills	οἱ λογαριασμοί ee logareeasmee		
the cups of tea			τά τσάγια ta tsaya
the glasses of beer		οἱ μπύρες ee beeress	
the keys			τά κλειδιά ta kleethya
the menus	οἱ κατάλογοι ee katalogee		
the newspapers		οἱ εφημερίδες ee efeemereethes	
the receipts		οἱ ἀποδείξεις ee apodeeksees	
the sandwiches			τά σάντουϊτς ta sandwich
the suitcases		οἱ βαλίτσες ee valeetses	
the telephone directories	οἱ τηλεφωνικοί κατάλογοι ee teelefoneekee katalogee		
the timetables			τά δρομολόγια ta thromologeea

Important things to remember

● In the plural: most masculine nouns end in -οι (ee)
   most feminine nouns end in -ες (ess) or -εις (eess)
   most neuter nouns end in -α (ah), -ια (ya), or -τα (tah)

● *the* in the plural is:
   οἱ (ee) before masculine and feminine nouns
   τά (tah) before neuter nouns

In phrases beginning: 'Have you got the . . .?'
                     'I'd like the . . .?'
                     'Where can I get the . . .?'

as in the singular, in the plural, Greek nouns and articles become the object of the sentence and change to form the accusative. Therefore:

	the	noun endings
masculine	οἱ (ee) becomes τούς (toos)	-οι (ee) becomes -ους (oos)
feminine	οἱ (ee) becomes τίς (tees)	(no change)
neuter	(no change)	(no change)

Practise saying and writing these sentences in Greek (masculine nouns are marked * to remind you that *both* the article and the nouns change but remember to change the article with feminine nouns).

Have you got the suitcases?	Ἔχετε τίς βαλίτσες;
	eheteh tees valeetsess
Have you got the keys?	Ἔχετε τά κλειδιά;
	eheteh ta kleethya
*Have you got the bills?	Ἔχετε τούς λογαριασμούς;
	eheteh toos logareeasmoos
I'd like the keys	Θά ἤθελα τά κλειδιά
	tha eethela ta kleethya
I'd like the timetables	Θά ἤθελα τά δρομολόγια
	tha eethela ta thromologeea
*I'd like the bills	Θά ἤθελα τούς λογαριασμούς
	tha eethela toos logareeasmoos
I'd like the newspapers	Θά ἤθελα τίς ἐφημερίδες
	thá eethela tees efeemereethess
Where can I get the keys?	Ποῦ μπορῶ νά βρῶ τά κλειδιά;
	poo boro na vro ta kleethya
Where can I get the newspapers?	Ποῦ μπορῶ νά βρῶ τίς ἐφημερίδες;
	poo boro na vro tees efeemereethess
Where can I get the suitcases?	Ποῦ μπορῶ νά βρῶ τίς βαλίτσες;
	poo boro na vro tees valeetsess

A/AN

a/an	masculine	feminine	neuter
an address		μία διεύθυνση meea thee-eftheensee	
an apple			ἕνα μῆλο enna meeloh
a bill	ἕνας λογαριασμός ennass logareeasmoss		
a cup of tea			ἕνα τσάι enna tsa-ee
a glass of beer		μία μπύρα meea beera	
a key			ἕνα κλειδί enna kleethee
a menu	ἕνας κατάλογος ennass katalogoss		
a newspaper		μία ἐφημερίδα meea efeemereetha	
a receipt		μία ἀπόδειξη meea apotheeksee	
a sandwich			ἕνα σάντουϊτς enna sandwich
a suitcase		μία βαλίτσα meea valeetsa	
a telephone directory	ἕνας τηλεφωνικός κατάλογος ennass teelefoneekoss katalogoss		
a timetable			ἕνα δρομολόγιο enna thromo-logee

Important things to remember

- *A* or *an* is ἕνας (ennass) before a masculine noun
  - μία (meea) before a feminine noun
  - ἕνα (enna) before a neuter noun
- *Some* or *any* is not translated in Greek, simply say the noun by itself e.g.
  - Have you got a key? Ἔχετε ἕνα κλειδί;
    - eheteh enna kleethee
  - Have you got (some) keys? Ἔχετε κλειδιά;
    - eheteh kleethya

In phrases beginning: Have you got a/some . . .?
                       I'd like a/some . . .?
                       Where can I get a/some . . .?

where Greek nouns and articles become the object of the sentence in the accusative, in the masculine only the word for *a/an* changes from ἕνας (ennass) to ἕνα (enna) and the noun endings change as before (see notes on *the* above). e.g. ἕνας λογαριασμός (ennass logareeasmoss) becomes ἕνα λογαριασμό (enna logareeasmoh).

Practise saying and writing these sentences in Greek (masculine nouns are marked * to remind you that *both* the article and the noun ending change).

Have you got a receipt?	Ἔχετε μία ἀπόδειξη; eheteh meea apotheeksee
*Have you got a menu?	Ἔχετε ἕνα κατάλογο; eheteh enna katalogo
*I'd like a telephone directory	Θά ἤθελα ἕνα τηλεφωνικό κατάλογο tha eethela enna teelefoneeko katalogo
I'd like some keys	Θά ἤθελα κλειδιά tha eethela kleethya
Where can I get some newspapers?	Ποῦ μπορῶ νά ἀγοράσω ἐφημερίδες; poo boro na agoraso efeemereethess
Where can I get a timetable?	Ποῦ μπορῶ νά βρῶ ἕνα δρομολόγιο; poo boro na vro enna thromologeeo
Is there a menu?	Ὑπάρχει ἕνας κατάλογος; eeparhee ennass katalogoss
Is there a key?	Ὑπάρχει ἕνα κλειδί; eeparhee enna kleethee
Is there a timetable?	Ὑπάρχει ἕνα δρομολόγιο; eeparhee enna thromologeeo
Are there any keys?	Ὑπάρχουν κλειδιά; eeparhoon kleethya
Are there any newspapers?	Ὑπάρχουν ἐφημερίδες; eeparhoon efeemereethess
Are there any sandwiches?	Ὑπάρχουν σάντουϊτς; eeparhoon sandwich

EXTRA PRACTICE WITH 'SOME'

Look at the list below:

the bread	τό ψωμί toh psom*ee*	some bread	ψωμί psom*ee*
the ice-cream	τό παγωτό toh pagot*oh*	some ice-cream	παγωτό pagot*oh*
the coffee	ὁ καφές o kaf*ess*	some coffee	καφέ ka*feh*
the sugar	ἡ ζάχαρη ee z*aharee*	some sugar	ζάχαρη z*aharee*
the water	τό νερό toh ner*oh*	some water	νερό ner*oh*
the wine	τό κρασί toh krass*ee*	some wine	κρασί krass*ee*

Practise saying and writing these sentences in Greek:

I'd like some bread	Θά ἤθελα ψωμί tha *ee*thela psom*ee*
I'd like some water	Θά ἤθελα νερό tha *ee*thela ner*oh*
Where can I buy some cheese?	Ποῦ μπορῶ νά ἀγοράσω τυρί; poo boro na agoraso teer*ee*
Where can I buy some ice-cream?	Ποῦ μπορῶ νά ἀγοράσω παγωτό; poo boro na agoraso pagoto
Where can I buy some aspirin?	Ποῦ μπορῶ νά ἀγοράσω ἀσπιρίνη; poo boro na agoraso aspeer*ee*nee
Have you got some coffee?	Ἔχετε καφέ; *eh*eteh kaf*eh*
Have you got some lemonade?	Ἔχετε λεμονάδα; *eh*eteh lemon*a*tha
Have you got some wine?.	Ἔχετε κρασί; *eh*eteh krass*ee*

THIS AND THAT

There are two words in Greek
αὐτό (this)
aft*o*
ἐκεῖνο (that)
ekeeno
If you don't know the Greek name for an object, just point and say:

Θά ἤθελα αὐτό/ἐκεῖνο	I'd like this/that
tha *eethela* aft*o*/ekeeno	

HELPING OTHERS

You can help yourself with phrases such as:

I'd like . . . a sandwich	Θά ἤθελα . . . ἕνα σάντουϊτς
	tha *eethela* . . . enna sandwich
Where can I get . . . a newspaper?	Ποῦ μπορῶ νά ἀγοράσω . . . μία ἐφημερίδα;
	poo boro na agora*so* . . . me*ea* efeemere*etha*
I need . . . a receipt	Χρειάζομαι . . . μία ἀπόδειξη
	hree-*azom*-eh . . . me*ea* apotheeksee

If you come across a compatriot having trouble making himself or herself understood, you should be able to speak to the Greek person on their behalf.

Note that it is not necessary to say the words for *he* αὐτός (aftos) *she* αὐτή (aftee) and *I* ἐγώ (egoh) in Greek unless you want to emphasise them e.g. *He'll* have a beer and *I'll* have a glass of wine.

He'd like a sandwich	Θά ἤθελε ἕνα σάντουϊτς
	tha *eethell*-eh enna sandwich
She'd like a sandwich	Θά ἤθελε ἕνα σάντουϊτς
	tha *eethell*-eh enna sandwich
Where can he get a newspaper?	Ποῦ μπορεῖ νά ἀγοράσει μία ἐφημερίδα;
	poo bor-*ee* na agora*ss*-ee me*ea* ef-eemehr-*eetha*

Where can she get a newspaper?	Ποῦ μπορεῖ νά ἀγοράσει μία ἐφημερίδα; poo bor-*ee* na agorass-ee m*ee*a ef-eemer-*ee*tha
He needs a receipt	Χρειάζεται μία ἀπόδειξη hree-*a*zet-eh m*ee*a apo-theek-see
She needs a receipt	Χρειάζεται μία ἀπόδειξη hree-*a*zet-eh m*ee*a apo-theek-see

You can also help a couple or a group if they are having difficulties. The Greek words for *they* are αὐτές (aftess) for women, αὐτοί (aftee) for men, but they are usually left out altogether. Look at the verb ending.

They'd like some cheese	Θά θέλανε τυρί tha thell-aneh teer-*ee*
Where can they get some aspirins?	Ποῦ μποροῦν νά ἀγοράσουν ἀσπιρίνες; poo bor-*oon* na agorass-*oon* aspeereen-ess
They need some water	Χρειάζονται νερό hree-*a*zon-deh neroh

What about the two of you? The word for *we* is ἐμεῖς (emeess) but what is really important is to change the verb ending.

We'd like some wine	Θά θέλαμε κρασί tha thellam-eh krass-*ee*
Where can we get some aspirins?	Ποῦ μποροῦμε νά ἀγοράσουμε ἀσπιρίνες: poo bor-*oom*-eh na agorass-*oom*-eh aspeereen-ess
We need a beer	Χρειαζόμαστε μία μπύρα hree-azom-asteh m*ee*a beer-a

Overleaf is a checklist for these useful phrase starters:

Θά ἤθελα ... tha *ee*thela	I'd like ...
Θά ἤθελε ... tha *ee*thel-eh	He'd/she'd like ...
Θά θέλαμε ... tha th*e*lam-eh	We'd like ...
Θά θέλανε ... tha th*e*l-aneh	They'd like ...
Ποῦ μπορῶ νά βρῶ ... poo bor*o* na vro	Where can I get ...?
Ποῦ μπορεῖ νά βρεῖ ... poo bor*ee* na vree	Where can he/she get ...?
Ποῦ μποροῦμε νά βροῦμε ... poo bor*oo*me na vr*oo*me	Where can we get ...?
Ποῦ μποροῦν νά βροῦν ... poo bor*oo*n na vroon	Where can they get ...?
Χρειάζομαι ... hree-*a*zom-eh	I need ...
Χρειάζεται ... hree-*a*zet-eh	He/she needs ...
Χρειαζόμαστε ... hree-*a*zom-asteh	We need ...
Χρειάζονται ... hree-*a*zon-deh	They need ...

MORE PRACTICE

Look at the opposite page and see how many different sentences you can make up, using the various points of information given earlier in this section.

	singular	plural
ashtray	τασάκι (n) tasahkee	τασάκια tasahkya
bag	τσάντα (f) tsanda	τσάντες tsandess
book	βιβλίο (n) veevleeo	βιβλία veevleea
car	αὐτοκίνητο (n) aftokeeneeto	αὐτοκίνητα aftokeeneeta
chair	καρέκλα (f) karehkla	καρέκλες karehkless
chemist	φαρμακείο (n) farmakeeo	φαρμακεία farmakeea
cigarette	τσιγάρο (n) tseegaro	τσιγάρα tseegara
driver	ὁδηγός (m) otheegoss	ὁδηγοί otheegee
fruit	φροῦτο (n) frootoh	φροῦτα frootah
glass	ποτήρι (n) poteeree	ποτήρια poteerya
ice-cream	παγωτό (n) pagoto	παγωτά pagota
olive	ἐλιά (f) ellya	ἐλιές ellyess
post-office	ταχυδρομείο (n) taheethromeeo	ταχυδρομεία taheethromeea
room	δωμάτιο (n) thomateeo	δωμάτια thomateea
salad	σαλάτα (f) salata	σαλάτες salatess
station	σταθμός (m) stathmoss	σταθμοί stathmee
telephone	τηλέφωνο (n) teelefono	τηλέφωνα teelefona
ticket	εἰσιτήριο (n) eeseeteerio	εἰσιτήρια eeseeteerya
tinned food	κονσέρβα (f) konserva	κονσέρβες konservess
tomato	ντομάτα (f) domata	ντομάτες domatess

Index

Notes

LANGUAGE AND TRAVEL BOOKS

Multilingual
The Insult Dictionary:
   How to Give 'Em Hell in 5 Nasty Languages
The Lover's Dictionary:
   How to be Amorous in 5 Delectable Languages
Multilingual Phrase Book
International Traveler's Phrasebook

Spanish
Vox Spanish and English Dictionaries
Harrap's Concise Spanish and English Dictionary
The Spanish Businessmate
Nice 'n Easy Spanish Grammar
Spanish Verbs and Essentials of Grammar
Getting Started in Spanish
Spanish Verb Drills
Guide to Spanish Idioms
Guide to Correspondence in Spanish
Español para los Hispanos
Diccionario Básico Norteamericano

French
Harrap's French and English Dictionaries
French Verbs and Essentials of Grammar
Getting Started in French
French Verb Drills
Guide to Correspondence in French
The French Businessmate
Nice 'n Easy French Grammar

German
New Schöffler-Weis German and English Dictionary
Klett German and English Dictionary
Harrap's Concise German and English Dictionary
Getting Started in German
German Verb Drills
German Verbs and Essentials of Grammar
The German Businessmate
Nice 'n Easy German Grammar

Italian
Getting Started in Italian

Russian
Russian Essentials of Grammar
Business Russian

Just Enough Books
Just Enough Dutch
Just Enough French
Just Enough German
Just Enough Greek
Just Enough Italian
Just Enough Japanese
Just Enough Portuguese
Just Enough Scandinavian
Just Enough Serbo-Croat
Just Enough Spanish

Just Listen 'n Learn Language Programs
Complete Courses in Spanish, French,
   German, Italian and Greek

Travel and Reference
Nagel's Encyclopedia Guides
World at Its Best Travel Series
Japan Today
British/American Language Dictionary
Bon Voyage!
Hiking and Walking Guide to Europe

 **PASSPORT BOOKS**

Trade Imprint of National Textbook Company
4255 West Touhy Avenue
Lincolnwood, Illinois 60646-1975 U.S.A.